# Studies in Modernity and National Identity

Sibel Bozdoğan and Reşat Kasaba
Series Editors

**Studies in Modernity and National Identity** examine the relationships among modernity, the nation-state, and nationalism as these have evolved in the nineteenth and twentieth centuries. Titles in this interdisciplinary and transregional series also illuminate how the nation-state is being undermined by the forces of globalization, international migration, electronic information flows, as well as resurgent ethnic and religious affiliations. These books highlight historical parallels and continuities while documenting the social, cultural, and spatial expressions through which modern national identities have been constructed, contested, and reinvented.

*Modernism and Nation Building: Turkish Architectural Culture in the Early Republic*
Sibel Bozdoğan

*Chandigarh's Le Corbusier: The Struggle for Modernity in Postcolonial India*
Vikramaditya Prakash

# Chandigarh's Le Corbusier

## The Struggle for Modernity in Postcolonial India

Vikramaditya Prakash

University of Washington Press

Seattle & London

*For Leah*

Publication of *Chandigarh's Le Chandigarh's* is supported by a grant from the Graham Foundation for Advanced Studies in the Fine Arts.

Published simultaneously in the United States and India by:

University of Washington Press
P.O. Box 50096, Seattle, WA 98145-5096

Mapin Publishing Pvt. Ltd.
31 Somnath Road, Usmanpura, Ahmedabad 380013

Library of Congress Cataloging-in-Publication Data
Prakash, Vikramaditya.
Chandigarh's Le Corbusier: the struggle for modernity in postcolonial India / Vikramaditya Prakash.
      p.  cm—(Studies in modernity and national identity)
        ISBN 0-295-98207-1 (alk. paper)
1. Architecture—India—Chandigarh—20th century. 2. City planning—India—Chandigarh—History—20th century. 3. Le Corbusier, 1887-1965. 4. Chandigarh (India)—Social conditions.  I. Title. II. Series.

NA1508.C44 P73 2002
720'.954'552—dc21                          2002024559

# Contents

# ACKNOWLEDGMENTS

This book has its origin in the life that was provided for me by my parents Savitri and Aditya Prakash, and that was put into context by my sisters Vandana Kumar and Chetna Purnami. To them I owe gratitude for simply making my world. But there can be no doubt that it was the countless hours I spent with Sandeep Virmani up on the Capitol Esplanade that set the real questions of this book in motion. To him my dedication remains perennial. The earliest draft of the manuscript was written in the form of a master's thesis at Cornell University, and for those days I am most grateful to Mark Jarzombek for his friendship and endless encouragement. From that period I also remain indebted to Derek Spitz, who, amongst a million other things, taught me how to write, and to Professor Dominick LaCapra, who set the example for critical thinking. Cornell also sent me to Franz Ziegler, who opened the door to Le Corbusier's aesthetic world for me.

The work on the Open Hand was done in partnership with John Biln and Ijlal Muzaffer at Arizona State University. At the University of Washington, John Benavente and Paul Davis were my trusty student assistants, and Jan Haag my eternally supportive and merciless first editor. Claus Seligmann and Alex Anderson were the first readers of the manuscript. Anne Vernez-Moudon presented me with the Le Corbusier Swiss franc, and Sergio Palleroni encouraged me to write the personalized prologues to each chapter. To them all belong my sincerest thanks.

To Michael Duckworth, the indefatigable acquisitions editor of the University of Washington Press, I owe my deep respect and gratitude for steadfastly believing in this manuscript. I am also grateful to Sibel Bozdoğan and Reşat Kasaba, the general editors of the series in which this book is published, for their insightful commentary that significantly improved the manuscript. It was Alexander Schlutz's excellent copyediting and Bipin Shah's resourceful publishing house in Ahmedabad that made this book real. I humbly thank them for doing their work so extremely well.

I also owe my respects and gratitude to Balkrishna V. Doshi, Gayatri C. Spivak, and Anthony D. King for their many spontaneous conversations and insights. In Chandigarh, I would like to acknowledge the support and encouragement of my friends Jaspreet Takher and Kultar Nat, as well as that of Professors I. J. S. Bakshi and Rajneesh Wattas of the Chandigarh College of Architecture. V. N. Singh and the staff of the Chandigarh Museum Archives went out of their way to help me find material in the archives, as did S. K. Midha, chief architect of the Chandigarh Administration.

I would also like to thank the staff of the Fondation Le Corbusier in Paris for their prompt and helpful responses to all my queries and requests.

A grant from the Graham Foundation for Advanced Studies in the Fine Arts and the Johnston Hastings Teaching Award of the College of Architecture and Urban Planning at the University of Washington were significant sources of funding for this book. Additional financial support was provided by Ron McCoy, director of the School of Architecture at Arizona State University, Jeffrey K. Ochsner, chair of the Department of Architecture at the University of Washington, and Jerry V. Finrow, dean of the College of Architecture and Urban Planning at the University of Washington. My thanks go to them all.

And special thanks to Leah and DZ just for being there.

Chandigarh's Le Corbusier

# The "East-West" Opposition in Chandigarh's Le Corbusier

Birthing, or beginning, is always difficult. And painful. Even though in hindsight one may not remember it as so. Indeed one may not even remember it; it may become an effaced memory. This is always the danger—and the promise.

This might help explain the difficulty and urgency underlying my writing of this book, which arises from a desire to excavate and come to terms with the forces that have shaped my life. I was born and brought up in Chandigarh—that artificial city of postcolonial India, the instant capital of a freshly severed and deeply wounded Indian East Punjab, whose off-the-shelf, imported modernity was freighted with much promise and expectation. As home, inasmuch as city-space graphs identity, Chandigarh was/is who I am. This book, ostensibly and primarily about the making of Chandigarh, is also about my own making.

I belong to the second generation of postcolonial Indians. In the early 1980s, when I was studying architecture in Chandigarh, the last of the city's great monuments, the Open Hand, was just being constructed. While I barely understood what it meant, I was a zealous defender of its significance.

My father, Aditya Prakash, was less enthusiastic. He belongs to the first generation of Chandigarh inhabitants—Salman Rushdie's infamous "midnight's children." At the stroke of the midnight hour, 14–15 August 1947, when India became independent, my father was on a ship on his way to England to study architecture. He might have lived his whole life in the U.K., had he not heard of Chandigarh. Working in a small architect's office in Glasgow, however lucrative the prospect, did not compare with the historical opportunity to help design a new capital city, commissioned personally by Jawaharlal Nehru, the celebrated first prime minister of independent India. The India of 1950 was set astir by Nehru's call to modernization, and his word was gospel.

Modernity, in the Nehruvian lexicon, meant the aggressive effort to catch up with the West. Large hydroelectric dams, iron and steel plants, airlines, and new cities were the order of the day. Thus it was that the educated, westernized elites of India were called upon to build the edifice of modern India. Committed to the cause, my father packed his bags—bought himself LPs of Gilbert and Sullivan's "The Mikado"—and after five years abroad, headed home.

When my father joined the team of architects and planners at the place where Chandigarh was to be built, there were only a handful of villages there, farming the fertile land that surrounded them. The site, selected by aerial reconnaissance, was an alluvial plain, gently sloping to the south, right at the foothills of the Himalayas. There were no roads, not even a train line, and certainly no electricity. Full of hubris, nevertheless, the Chandigarh team—four from Europe, nine from India—set camp on that vast plain to plan and realize a grand vision of modernity.

This book is mostly about the strange apparitions that have arisen from this grand vision. It is also about hero-worship. The world-famous French modernist, Le Corbusier, was chosen as the chief architect of Chandigarh, or the Architectural Advisor to the Government of Punjab, as he was officially called.[1] He was the chief hero of Chandigarh. If my father was just beginning, Le Corbusier, already the well-established doyen of modernism, was in his prime. With a long litany of built and unbuilt projects behind him, Le Corbusier set to designing Chandigarh with well-rehearsed strokes. The Master Plan, the fables declaim, was prepared in a scant forty-eight hours. The rest was just detailing.

This experience, of helping design on such a massive scale working under the authoritative I/eye of Le Corbusier, was formative in my father's life. While my father had come to Le Corbusier to learn from him, the latter was on a crusade, intent on seeing his visions through, and had little time for his subordinates. Usually my father received his instructions through an intermediary. The privilege of working directly with Le Corbusier came rarely, and the Indian architects and planners had to compete to be able to do so.

The single major project on which my father directly worked with Le Corbusier was that of a School of Art, late in the 1950s, almost at the end of the Chandigarh Project. The design for the school had been languishing, and so my father made one of his own initiative and presented it to Le Corbusier. "Where is the système?" The Master asked as he dismissed the design in one glance. "Meet me tomorrow at your blackboard," he instructed, "then I will show you how to design." Le Corbusier had painted one wall in his own Atelier in Paris with blackboard paint, and my father had imitated him. The next day, my father, chalk and triangle in hand, drew up the whole design of the school on the wall, from plan to fenestration detail—while Le Corbusier sat on a stool and dictated dimensions. Communicated to him like a revelation, those dimensions my father can still recite from memory.[2]

Once one has worked under a "Master," one can spend the rest of one's life trying to break free from under there. In other contexts, this is also known as the postcolonial condition. Years later, as a practicing architect, painter, and principal of the Chandigarh College of Architecture (where I studied), my father was compelled to work through this legacy of having helped conceive a master city and having worked with a "Master." He would often repeat to his students, "I learnt everything I did from Le Corbusier—even if it was in going against everything he stood for." He has written three books, and produced elaborate plans of his own utopian city, in order to establish his own voice.

The relationship between Le Corbusier and all his supporters in India, including Jawaharlal Nehru, was not that different. A complete generation of Indian architects expended its energies trying to redefine itself, "after the masters." There is even a book on modern Indian architecture with that title.[3] As a second generation architect from Chandigarh, trained in the "Le Corbusier style," my writing of this book is certainly also about coming to terms with my legacy. But then, Nehru's India of the 1950s was also scrambling to define itself against a more advanced West. Perhaps that is the perennial dilemma of every new generation, the feeling of always being the latecomer to the main event. That is also what the "post" in postcolonial refers to.

*Long years ago we made a tryst with destiny, and now the time comes when we shall redeem our pledge, not wholly or in full measure, but very substantially. At the stroke of the midnight hour, when the world sleeps, India will awake to life and freedom. A moment comes which comes but rarely in history, when we step out from the old to the new, when an age ends, and when the soul of a nation, long suppressed, finds utterance. It is fitting that at this solemn moment we take the pledge of dedication to India and her people and to the still larger cause of humanity.*

*—Jawaharlal Nehru, first prime minister of independent India; speech given to the constituent assembly at midnight on 14–15 August 1947, when India became independent.*

On 14–15 August 1947, at the stroke of the midnight hour, when Pakistan and India became independent after two hundred years of colonial rule, their triumph was marred by religious communal violence. The departing British had decided to partition colonial India to create a new country—Pakistan—intended to safeguard the future of the Muslim minority. Six hundred years of Muslim rule had resulted in the conversion of roughly a quarter of India's 400 million inhabitants to Islam. They were spread everywhere, intricately woven into the social textile of India's cities and villages. Now they were deemed distinct and incompatible, and ordained to be separated into their own country. The desire to catalogue and classify had always been a hallmark of British colonial administration. It imparted a sense of order. The partition was its final outcome, and in a certain sense, its logical conclusion.

In June 1947, Sir Cyril Radcliffe, a well-known English barrister, was chosen for the unenviable task of re-drawing the colonial map. He knew little about India and had no history of any association with things Indian. That is precisely why he was chosen, to project his impartiality. His task was to slough off two sections, separated by a thousand miles, and call them Pakistan. The various princes, who were nominally independent, were left to choose their own affiliations.

The lives of 88 million people were directly affected by the partition. As the news spread, and the partitioning maps were known, millions of Muslims and non-Muslims suddenly found themselves on the wrong side of the dividing line, in the wrong cities and villages. They were given seventy-three days to prepare for their new lives. More than 13 million left their homes, packed what little they could take, and headed for their new countries as refugees.[4]

En route, more than a million people were massacred by their counterparts in a series of bloody reprisals. The causes of what is now called "ethnic violence" are diverse. While reprisals have a way of gathering momentum entirely on their own, centuries of Hindu-Muslim neighborly co-existence must also have nurtured deep layers of resentment and distrust. At the anxious hour of an uncertain future, the official certification of difference as irreconcilable and absolute may have served as a scapegoat, a vent for fears and anxieties.

The states of Bengal and Punjab were those worst hit. They were partitioned through the middle, into East Bengal (Pakistan) and West Bengal (India), and into West Punjab (Pakistan) and East Punjab (India). In West Bengal's largest city, Calcutta, the violence wore on. Mahatma Gandhi, the chief architect of India's nonviolent path to freedom, started the sixteenth of his famous protest fasts. He swore not to eat until all the violence stopped in the city. At seventy-seven, Gandhi's body was frail and declined fast. But his strategy worked, yet again. After three days, as local Hindu and Muslim leaders gathered around Gandhi, the city became silent. The slaughter ceased, but thousands already had been murdered.[5]

Punjab was not so fortunate. Nehru sent the military out to escort the overcrowded trains laden with refugees that were coming over the border. But they were largely ineffective. Untempered by a Gandhian miracle, in Punjab tens of thousands more were killed, and millions were left refugees bereft not only of their erstwhile homelands, but often of their extended families and livelihoods as well.

It was in the immediate aftermath of partition, for reasons both practical and symbolic, that Chandigarh was conceived. While West Bengal retained the new colonial city of Calcutta, East Punjab, quid pro quo, surrendered Lahore, its ancient capital, to Pakistan. Lahore was one of the old economic and cultural centers established by the Mughals in the seventeenth century. For three hundred years it had been the center of the Punjab. Now it was capital to only half the state, on the Pakistan side.

Immediately after independence, the government of Indian East Punjab (henceforth simply "Punjab"), which was already coping with a gigantic refugee problem, also had to start functioning without an administrative center and capital city. While temporary lodging for the government was found in Shimla, the hill-station that was the old summer capital of the colonial government, a hunt to determine a new capital for the state was immediately undertaken by the State Government. The most expedient and cost-effective solution was to adopt an existing city as the new capital and simply build new legislative buildings. Many were proposed. Amritsar, the largest Punjabi city with the revered Sikh shrine the Golden Temple, was the logical choice, but it was deemed to be too close to the Pakistani border and therefore vulnerable to attack. Patiala, another erstwhile capital to a Punjabi dynasty, was another possibility, but it was perceived to be geographically too removed from the heart of Punjab. Ambala, a relatively new British military cantonment, was also considered, but it was thought to be too small and insignificant to project the image of a capital worthy of replacing Lahore.

In March 1948, the government of Punjab, in spite of numerous cautions against the enormous expenditure involved, finally decided to build a new capital city for itself. Not much is documented about the exact logic of the decision, but Nehru's opinion on the matter was clearly instrumental. For Nehru, the rehabilitation of Punjab, both practical and symbolic, required the making of a grand new city. He chastised the State Government for delaying the decision:

> Right from September 1947 the Government of India has been laying great stress on the urgency of this matter from every point of view, practical as well as psychological. In a sense the rehabilitation of East Punjab centers round it and yet because of doubt and uncertainty and repeated changes of policy and decision, nothing so far has been finalized. … To go on waiting for large grants from the Centre is not a worthwhile policy. … I would strongly suggest to you to go ahead with this matter even though you do not get any financial support from the Centre.[6]

In the end, according to P. L. Verma, the chief engineer of Punjab, the critical reason to build a new city was not practical but symbolic. "None of the existing cities of Punjab," he recalled, "possessed sufficient magnificence and glamour to make up for the psychological loss of Lahore suffered by the strife-stricken but proud Punjabis."[7]

A true child of the midnight hour, Chandigarh was thus encumbered with great expectations. "Like the rising of the Phoenix from the ashes of its own fire" was the slogan of the motley group of architects, engineers, and bureaucrats from three continents that was assembled to build the city.[8] Retrospectively, one can sense that the hubris of independence must have been invested with gusto in an attempt to nullify the disaster of partition.

## Nehru's Postcolonial Modern

With the decision to make a new capital in place, the work of actually making Chandigarh was undertaken with a sense of urgency. A site for the project was selected right away, but in mid-1949 it was changed to its present location in an effort to reduce the number of people that the project would displace. Even so, twenty-four villages and 9,000 residents were forced to give up their land and relocate. They actively protested their displacement, but the project went forward, driven by the optimism and determination of the central government (fig. 1.1).

Chandigarh was named after one of the existing villages, which had a temple dedicated to the Hindu goddess Chandi. Chandi-garh means the abode/stronghold of Chandi, who is a manifestation of Shakti, the ubiquitous female principle in the Hindu cosmogony. As time proceeds through its inevitable and recurrent circles of creation and destruction, Chandi is the energy, the enabling force of transformation and change. Her participation, in one form or another, is mandatory at all events of any significance. The inherent auspiciousness of her presence must surely not have escaped the Hindu officials who picked the site.[9]

This Chandi temple still exists, but remains un-remarked and un-noticed since it is located on the outskirts of Chandigarh, and is in no way integrated into the general

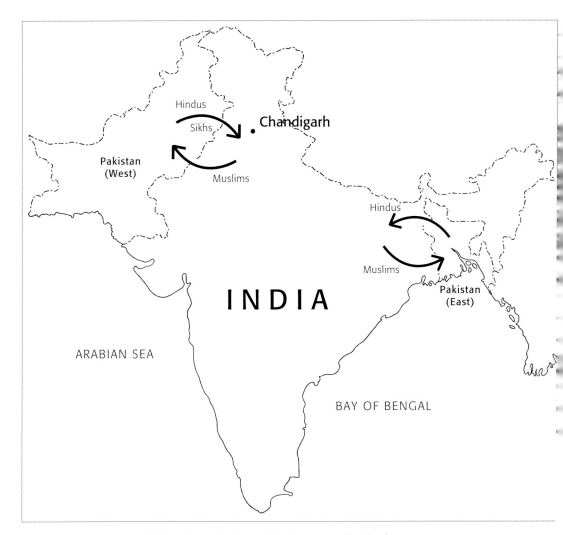

**Fig. 1.1** Map showing the 1947 partition of India and the location of Chandigarh.

master plan or architecture of the city. This is no doubt because the blinding commandment that defined Chandigarh's identity from its very inception was that it had to be a "modern" city. With finely crafted oratory, at the inaugural ceremony of Chandigarh, Nehru declared grandly: "Let this be a new city, unfettered by the traditions of the past, a symbol of the nation's faith in the future."[10]

In Nehru's grand plan, Chandigarh had to reflect the modern aspirations of the new Indian nation. Nehru's views of development differed significantly from those of his mentor, Mahatma Gandhi. While both of them agreed that colonization had resulted in the destruction of indigenous industries and livelihoods, they differed considerably on the critical question of what was to be done next. Gandhi, influenced by Ruskin, Thoreau, and Tolstoy, considered industrialization to be an evil in itself and wanted the self-sustaining village to be the fundamental economic and social unit of the new nation. Nehru wanted to pursue aggressive industrialization, controlled by a centralized welfare state, to catch up with the developments of the West. With Gandhi's death in January 1948—early in the history of the new Indian nation—the Nehruvian doctrine prevailed.

For Nehru, modernity and Chandigarh had to be inextricably yoked to a vision for the future. He sent out a clear signal. Although it was meant to replace the ancient city of Lahore, there was to be no place for nostalgia in Chandigarh. He did not want an existing old city to embody the new nation because he believed that oldness, with its overwhelming weight of tradition, held India down. Deeply influenced by colonial perceptions, Nehru was convinced that it was static traditional practices, which had not adequately responded to change, that had caused India's colonization. In a seminar on architecture in 1957, he clearly spelled out his position:

> [The previous speaker] referred to the static condition in regard to architecture in India during the last two, three hundred years. That really was a reflex of the static condition of the Indian mind or Indian conditions. Everything was static—there are bright individuals and bright movement but taken as a whole India was static. In fact, India was static before that. In fact, without being very accurate or precise, architecturally considered, for the last few hundred years, India was static and the great buildings which we admire really date back to a considerable time. Even before the British came, we had become static. In fact, the British came because we are static. A society which ceases to change ceases to go ahead, necessarily becomes weak and it is an extraordinary thing how that weakness comes out in all forms of creative activity.[11]

Nehru's prescription for overcoming this "weakness" in Indian society, was the invigoration of a massive state-sponsored project of modernization. An admirer of both the United States and the Soviet Union, Nehru strove to amalgamate the best of both these nations in India. On the Soviet model, he set up gigantic mining and manufacturing public-sector undertakings, and initiated the system of five-year national development plans. At the same time, Nehru was totally committed to democratic principles and valored education as the route to emancipation. To generate new knowledge and expertise, he developed a series of scientific, educational, and cultural institutions.[12] Modeling his state practices on Roosevelt's New Deal, he ordered the construction of numerous Tennessee Valley Authority–inspired hydroelectric dam projects. The most famous of these was the Bhakra Nangal Dam, located not far from Chandigarh, destined not only to supply water and electricity to the city, but to be inextricably intertwined with its history.

By professed ideology, however, modernization for Nehru was not just a question of style or identity, or of doing things as they were done in the West. Rather, as the antidote to stasis, it was an attitude, a tremendous churning of creative minds:

> The main thing today is that a tremendous amount of building is taking place in India and an attempt should be made to give it a right direction and to encourage creative minds to function with a measure of freedom so that new types may come out, new designs, new types, new ideas, and out of that amalgam something new and good will emerge.[13]

The inherent value of the new, in Nehru's view, simply was that it was "a measure of freedom," liberated from the stasis of history. To be modern was to be new, and the New and the Good, in the Nehruvian semantics, were synonymous. Furthermore, fresh out of the violence of partition, Nehru was convinced that by focusing on modernity he could sidestep the pitfalls of ancient identities. As Kemal Ataturk had done in Turkey, and as other postcolonial nations like Brazil and Nigeria had aspired to do, Nehru hoped that the newly independent Indian population would sufficiently identify itself with the idea of modernity, re-invent itself, and thereby avoid the continued specter of ethnic violence. If modernism was his new religion, then newness and change were its gospel.

This is the context in which Nehru proclaimed the hydroelectric projects to be the "temples of modern India." And it is this context in which we can understand Nehru's dictum for Chandigarh: "Let this be a new city unfettered by the traditions of the past, and a symbol of the nation's faith in the future." Chandigarh was not to be "unfettered by the traditions of the past" *and* a "symbol of the nation's faith in the future"; rather, the new capital was to symbolize that faith in the future *by* being unfettered by the traditions of the past. Furthermore, I would argue that Nehru's Chandigarh was not meant to be a prophesy of the future, as was subsequently assumed by the various planners who adopted its planning principles for other cities, but was intended as an expression of faith in the future—the belief that the modern way of thinking and doing things would allow the future to emerge. His investment in modernization, in other words, was instrumental—as a catalyst for change.

Ultimately, therefore, Nehru was dedicated to the precipitation of a wholly original and new vision for India that was its very own, and even better and beyond those of the outside world from which it had derived its first models. The outstanding manifestations of this Nehruvian hope was his foreign policy, where he conceived and formed the Non-Aligned Movement, that was designed to sidestep the destructive bipolar choices of the Cold War in favor of a third alternative that was far more human and rational. The world of the 1950s lived in constant fear of the nuclear threat, and for Nehru to propose a radical alternative from the platform of a relatively weak and defenseless country, was both courageous and supremely optimistic. Nonetheless, those were Nehru's expectations for his modernist aspirations.

This transformative vision of modernism was of course predicated on his perception of India as being static and effete. This perception was a consequence of the internalization of the experience of colonization. Of the various stereotypes of colonial ideology, perhaps none was as pervasive, and persuasive, as the projection that it was a modern, enlightened, and dynamic young West that had succeeded in colonizing and dominating an ancient, superstitious, venerable but effete, desirable but corrupt India—a result of its unfortunate entanglement with a decrepit and dysfunctional past.[14]

From the West's point of view, the colonial mission was legitimized as sharing the fruits of Enlightenment, spreading "universal" principles of liberty, equality, democracy, reason, science, etc. The inherent political contradiction between the egalitarian objectives of the Enlightenment and the hegemonic character of colonization was justified as the only way to deliver the colony into modernity, that might otherwise remain hobbled by the weight of tradition. This contradiction was romanticized as the "white man's burden."

The modernism of the postcolonial Nehruvian state, then, was the reciprocal response of the colonized, the self-empowering act of dissolving contradiction by simultaneously rejecting and appropriating the unsolicited gift of colonization. For Nehru, the repudiation of the colonizer did not also entail the repudiation of the promises of the colonial enterprise. When Nehru proclaimed that Chandigarh must be a modern city, his claim was not different in substance from that made earlier by the colonist. But since it was made by Nehru in the name of an independent nation state, it was fundamentally different in form, and thereby, in legitimacy. The ideological motivation behind the making of modern new cities in numerous post-colonies, such as Brasilia in Brazil, Islamabad in Pakistan, and Sher-e-Bangla Nagar in Bangladesh, was similar in nature.

Modernization, thus, was a mimicry of the colonial project, of the aims and aspirations of colonization, imitated and re-legitimized by the English-educated, Indian elite. If Orientalism was a discourse of the Orient, by and for the Occident; nationalism was its stepsister, a mimicry of the Occident, by and for the post-colony. It was, in this sense, the quintessential postcolonial project.

Mimicry and imitation, however, do not ensure that the end product will always be identical to the original. Quite the contrary. Mimic-men always have their own understanding of what they are mimicking—they see the world through their own interpretive lenses. That is what they aim to highlight. Thus while they may all agree on what they are imitating, the imitations can be significantly different and even contradictory.

In addition, the representatives of the originals, the standard-bearers of the West in our case, always claim ownership of the real truth of the content: the "true" goals of modernization. This is their legacy of the colonial experience—their continuing burden of the civilizing mission. In the postcolonial context however, it runs the heightened risk of being clouded by flattery, since the "natives" are now perceived to be acting entirely of their own volition—voluntarily admiring the West.

All this makes for great expectations, greater possibilities of disappointment, and much confusion. Such is the story of the making of Chandigarh.

### Translating the Nehruvian Vision into Architecture

The difficult task of translating Nehru's lofty expectation of Chandigarh, as of India, fell to functionaries of the state, the bureaucrats and the politicians, who mostly relied on foreign models and experts to show the way. In fact, the all-important decision to make Chandigarh according to an early twentieth-century English utopian urban planning model, was made by the first bureaucrat put in charge of the capital project, A. L. Fletcher. The city's first architect-planners, the Americans Albert Mayer and Matthew

**Fig. 1.2** The Secretariat. (Photograph by Philip Lehn)

Nowicki, were handed a brief that not only detailed the extremely low densities and the individualized bungalows that were required, but also explicitly cited the Garden City Movement as the principal ideology that was to be manifested in Chandigarh.

But, of course, it was the city's second team of architects and planners, hired after the unexpected death of Nowicki in 1950, who are remembered best for their association with Chandigarh. This was the team led by Le Corbusier (1887-1965), the famous Swiss-French architect, the man whose name is canonized as a central figure in the history of modern architecture. He was the author of the Master Plan, and the vast Capitol Complex, where the major institutions of state are located—the High Court, Legislative Assembly, Secretariat, and the unbuilt Governor's Residence (fig. 1.2; plates 1 and 2). In addition, he prepared the guidelines for the commercial center, and in an adjoining sector, he built a museum and a school of art.

The majority of the buildings within the city (other than those developed privately) were designed by Pierre Jeanneret, Maxwell Fry, and Jane Drew, assisted by a design team of nine Indian architects and planners. Jeanneret was Le Corbusier's cousin, and had been brought into the project by the latter, as the full-time resident architect.

**Fig. 1.3** Type 9F housing by Maxwell Fry.

Besides supervising Le Corbusier's buildings, Jeanneret designed a number of the larger housing types of Chandigarh, and also many of the important administrative buildings such as the administrative center of the University, the State Library and the Estate Office. The English husband and wife team of Fry and Drew was responsible for most of the government housing in Chandigarh. The job of the nine Indians—M. N. Sharma, A. R. Prabhawalkar, B. P. Mathur, Piloo Moody, U. E. Chowdhury, N. S. Lamba, Jeet Lal Malhotra, J. S. Dethe, and Aditya Prakash—was essentially to assist the foreign team, although in time they were given projects of their own. The huge engineering team assigned to execute the project was headed by P. L. Verma, while P. N. Thapar served as chief administrator.

Housing designs for Sectors 22 and 23 were the first to be developed. As most of Chandigarh's original housing was intended for government employees, it was decided that the housing construction costs would be determined by a set percentage of a government employee's income. Accordingly, Jeanneret, Fry, and Drew devised 13 (later 14) "types" of housing based on a spectrum of incomes from those of employees earning less than Rs. 50 per month to that of the Chief Minister (figs. 1.3, 1.4). Each design was given a designation with a number (denoting the economic sector for which

**Fig. 1.4** Special type 1E housing by Pierre Jeanneret and B. P. Mathur.

it was envisioned) paired with a letter (indicating the architect who designed it): Type 13J or 14M, for example. All the designs were visibly "modern," exhibiting stark geometries broken only by sunscreening devices like deep overhangs and recesses, perforated screens and open verandahs. There was even a "frame-control" system devised to regulate all the construction that was privately developed.

Chandigarh was originally designed for a population of 500,000. Fifty years after its birth, it already had a population of 900,000—almost double its anticipated size—while large satellite towns, Panchkula and S.A.S. Nagar, have developed just beyond the administrative boundaries of the city. In the years to come, the larger Chandigarh metropolitan area is expected to be home to a population of almost 2 million.

## Nehru and Le Corbusier

Of all the architects, however, it is Le Corbusier's name that is most famously associated with Chandigarh. One of the icons of utopian modernism, Le Corbusier embodied the image of the hero-architect, battling against the fortresses of old, forging a brave new world, whatever the odds. By the time he came to India, his books were well known and his skyscrapered cities, pristine and precise, were an integral part of the daily palette of the modern movement in architecture, not only in Europe but in North and South America as well. Even though none was actually built, they embodied futuristic thinking, with a straight-lined, no-nonsense style that connoted visions of high scientific rationality and mechanized perfection. Le Corbusier had the reputation of being both the standard bearer as well as an iconoclast, and his designs for some of the most prestigious twentieth-century projects, such as the League of Nations and the United Nations building, were simultaneously controversial and established icons of the modern movement in architecture. For Nehru's call for modernity, there could have been no better respondent, even though, as we shall later learn, Le Corbusier's choice as the chief architect and planner of Chandigarh was essentially accidental and last minute.

By the 1950s, when Le Corbusier came to Chandigarh, he was still very much a visionary, but was far from the technology-modernist that his reputation presaged. He was, indeed, a somewhat jaded man. Although modern architecture was closely identified with his person, Le Corbusier considered its true mission irreparably compromised. Modern life, driven by greed and profit, had, according to him, come disconnected from what he called the "fundamental facts" of nature. His ideal of the modern man was derived from a Rousseauesque image of the noble savage, an innocent in a pastoral world, uncorrupted by civilization.[15] He considered it the true mission of modern architecture to reestablish the aesthetic and poetic forms necessary for the liberation and deliverance of this modern man. This involved thinking of architecture as a technology, quite literally a machine that enables daily human life to be in harmony with the stars, the sun, the earth, the rivers, and other forces of nature.

At its core, Le Corbusier's mission was redemptive and eschatological, and Chandigarh was, in his expectation, his true, and possibly last, opportunity to achieve his objective. There seemed to be a vindication at hand:

> India, that humane and profound civilization … At the end of the race, 1951 at
> Chandigarh contact [is] possible with the essential joys of the Hindu principle:
> brotherhood, relationship between the cosmos and living things: Stars, nature, sacred
> animals, birds, monkeys, and cows, and in the village children, adults and old people,
> the pond and the mango trees, everything is present and … poor but proportioned.[16]

"Poor but proportioned"—Le Corbusier's enchantment with India's "humane and profound civilization," far from leading him to question the need to even modernize, only served to reassure him of the veracity of his vision of a true modernism:

> India has, and always has had a peasant culture that exists since a thousand years! … But
> India has not yet created an architecture for modern civilization (offices, factories,
> buildings). India is suddenly jumping into the second era of mechanization. Instead of
> sinking into the gropings and errors of the first era we will be able to fulfill our mission;
> give India the architecture of modern times.[17]

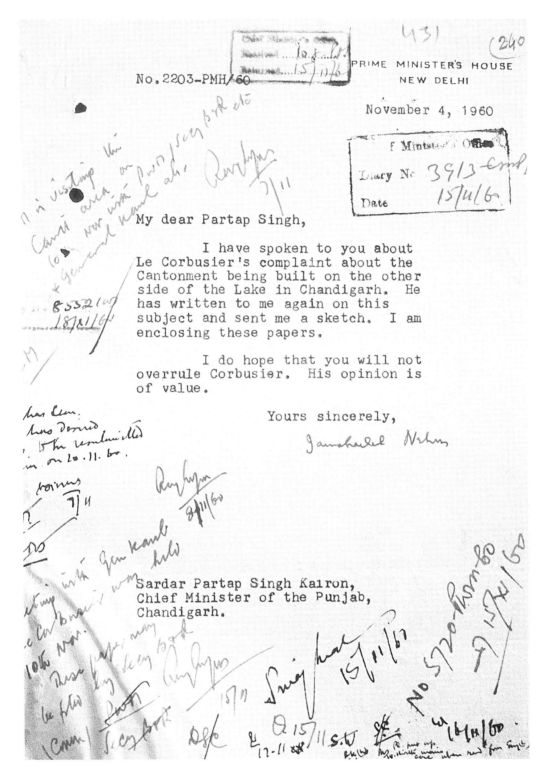

Fig. 1.5 Nehru's letter on behalf of Le Corbusier, written to the chief minister of Punjab.
(Chandigarh Museum Archives)

As we know, however, Le Corbusier had not been invited to India to celebrate the bucolic possibilities of the "Hindu" agrarian culture. Rather he had been expressly charged with the mission to embody a third world nation's self-conscious visions and aspirations for the future. For Nehru, the India of 1947, with its villages and bullock carts, was not a picture of the "essential joys" of life. Rather it was the embodiment of the desolation and backwardness that had led to two hundred years of colonial rule, that had prevented India from participating in the forward march of modernity.

The situation therefore was fraught with contradictions. Although Le Corbusier and Nehru agreed that Chandigarh had to be a "modern" city, and cemented a close friendship around that agreement, their outlooks never quite melded (fig. 1.5). While Le Corbusier's modernism was nostalgic of a poor and primitivistic India, Nehru's modernism aspired to an unbridled liberalization from the shackles of poverty and primitivism. For Nehru, under the influence of colonization, modernism was a strategic catalyst of growth and change—the West on tap rather than on top. For Le Corbusier on the other hand, Chandigarh was his opportunity to fulfill the unrealized potential of an ideological investment—the resuscitation of a dying modernism through an old fantasy.

In this book, I have tracked some of the ways in which the ideals and objectives of the two men both converged and diverged. Their congruence was obvious. Modern men of the same persuasion, both of them considered the question of making an "Indian" or "European" architecture as obsolete and pointless and the solution was to be found through fundamental investigations. For Nehru, for instance, Le Corbusier's buildings in Chandigarh were above cultural identification. "It is wrong to call the new buildings European," he railed, "these just reflect the changed environments, the industrial age, the new social order and the modern scientific technological advances." "It is good that the idea of Chandigarh is spreading," he continued. "It is good that architects are concerning themselves with the problems of new materials at their disposal and are thinking of such things as light, air, water, landscape, civic needs and human beings."[18]

Behind their professed faiths in modernity lay their divergent desires for the Other; for Le Corbusier the longing for the primitive, for Nehru the lure of the material and ideological transformation. An outstanding story, characterizing their similarities and differences is that of the Open Hand monument that Le Corbusier proposed for Chandigarh and atop the Bhakra Nangal Dam, Nehru's largest hydroelectric power project. Le Corbusier designed the Hand with an elegant and dramatic silhouette, and proposed it as the symbol of Nehru's foreign policy brainchild, the Non-Aligned Movement. While "the modern world is torn between the USA and the URSS (sic)," Le Corbusier wrote to Nehru in a letter dated 22 July 1955, that

> the Asiatic East is gathering together… This monument will have far reaching ethical consequences. I am sure that by dressing in this place "the Open Hand," India will make a gesture which will corroborate your intervention which is so decisive at the crucial moment of the machinist evolution and its threats.[19]

The "intervention" that Le Corbusier was offering to corroborate was the famous Afro-Asian Conference that was held in Bandung, Indonesia, in April 1955. (Le Corbusier's letter was written soon after in July 1955.) This conference, essentially designed to bring together the countries of Asia and Africa, most of which had been recently liberated from colonization, became extraordinarily important because it represented the peak of the rivalry between India and China for moral, intellectual, and political leadership of the non-aligned world. At the Bandung conference a friendship was cemented between Jawaharlal Nehru, Gamal Abdel Nasser, president of Egypt (1956–70) and Marshall Josip Broz Tito, president of Yugoslavia (1956-80). These three went on to formalize the Non-Aligned Movement in 1961. Beyond power-bloc politics, the Movement embodied the spirit of a third alternative beyond the two of the Cold War. As I mentioned earlier, the Movement was at the very heart of Nehru's beliefs and aspirations, and by some accounts it could be his best remembered legacy.

And yet, in spite of Le Corbusier's repeated letters to Nehru imploring him to have the Hand constructed, the latter refused to have it built, because it had been tarnished as a symbol by a series of local political events. For Le Corbusier, the Hand was a symbol of an eternal faith that endured in the face of all opposition. But for Nehru, the same Hand was only a proposed symbol whose relevance had passed. It took another thirty years after the death of both Le Corbusier and Nehru, before the meaning of the Hand was sufficiently diluted that it could be adopted by the Chandigarh Administration essentially for its graphic qualities.

In the end, then, secondary political considerations may have outweighed shared ideological dispensations. The record suggests that Nehru's support of Le Corbusier's architecture was fundamentally strategic. In a speech to the Indian Institute of Engineers, Nehru noted that he in fact did not like all the buildings there, but that Chandigarh was nevertheless an experiment that he "welcomed" considerably:

> Now I have welcomed very greatly, one experiment … Chandigarh. Many people argue about it, some like it, some dislike it. It is totally immaterial whether you like it or not. It is the biggest thing in India of this kind. That is why I welcome it. It is the biggest thing because it hits you on the head and makes you think. You may squirm at the impact but it makes you think and imbibe new ideas, and the one thing that India requires in so many fields is to be hit on the head so that you may think. …
>
> I do not like every building in Chandigarh. I like some very much, I like the general conception of the township very much but what I like above all, is this creative approach not being tied down to what has been done by our forefathers and the like but thinking out in new terms, trying to think in terms of light and air and ground and water and human beings, not in terms of rules and regulations laid down by our ancestors.[20]

Le Corbusier, in a somewhat different way, was just as strategic about accepting Nehru's support. On the one hand, Le Corbusier often portrayed Nehru as something of an exemplar, a political client of a different order: "Well, [in India] I was given the honor and joy of becoming the friend of Nehru, who is a great mind. He died unfortunately; however, he always supported me. I didn't have any conflicts in India. … They are correct in their dealings. … There are enemies, of course, but they're beaten from the start."[21]

Whenever Le Corbusier encountered opposition to his ideas in Chandigarh, he immediately dashed off a letter to Nehru, invoking him as "a friend" to intervene on his behalf. Nonetheless, Le Corbusier did not consider himself to be a simple translator of Nehru's commandments. In one of his letters to Nehru, Le Corbusier uses the metaphor of weight to characterize his work as his architect—to make the politician's speeches "concrete":

> To begin such a work [i.e., the making of Chandigarh by Le Corbusier] to spend days and years and sleepless nights on it. To take on all the responsibilities. It is no longer speeches which are weighed according to the music of the words. It's concrete which has to hold up, resist, and serve. And it's dangerous. (3#460)

One can interpret this quotation to mean that Le Corbusier saw his work in Chandigarh as that of concretizing Nehru's political ideals, both literally and figuratively. But given the weight of Le Corbusier's invectives against politicians, it could also mean the reverse: after Nehru's speeches, Le Corbusier had to do the real work, make things concrete.

Leader or led? Le Corbusier definitely saw himself as the leader of the flock; but he also liked to project himself as the working ass who simply carries the load, gets the job done. His life was replete with instances when he would challenge institutional authorities by parodic inversions. On one occasion, when he was being granted an honorary doctorate, Le Corbusier in his sketchbook characterized the chancellor of the University, the "consacre," who was going to give the doctorate to him, as a "sacre con," or "sacred ass." (4#374) Here, Le Corbusier, in a typical reversal, transforms the sacred into the profane. This court jester-like figure of the "sacred ass" is, I would like to argue, how Le Corbusier saw his own role as an architect, and the role of art in general. The court jester, like art, enjoys the unique privilege of being able to challenge authority without having to pay the consequences for his defiance. Although the jester challenges in jest, the jest can be serious. "Only those who play," Le Corbusier once wrote, "are serious types. … The mountain climbers, the rugby player and the card players, and the gamblers, are all frauds, for they do not play."[22] Le Corbusier loved reading Cervantes and Rabelais, constantly carried them with him, and on one occasion noted that he saw himself as a modern day Don Quixote, a "man of action" charging the windmills of established authority. (3#319)

Simultaneously leader and led, Le Corbusier saw his relationship with Nehru as a strategic alliance, predicated not so much on a meeting of minds as on the sharing of common goals, and on his role as the honest translator of those goals.

The making of Chandigarh, for both Nehru and Le Corbusier, thus was dedicated to a single problematic—the precipitation of a truly "modern Indian" architecture—and for both the answers to their aspirations lay in a postponed faith in tomorrow. Yet their visions were trained elsewhere, they saw different things. Nehru's and Le Corbusier's mirrored modernist recognition and confirmation of each other was, in other words, attended by a misrecognition. And although they were referring to the same object, ultimately the modernism that was imported by Nehru was not the same as the modernism that was exported by Le Corbusier. There are, therefore, at least two modernisms differentially woven into the single textile of Chandigarh.[23] Between Le Corbusier's modernism and that of Jawaharlal Nehru, as between Le Corbusier's "Western" background and Chandigarh's "Eastern" contexts, then, there was a lot of distance, ample opportunity for misrecognitions and misunderstandings and the inevitable need for negotiations.

## Critical Historiography

As the largest built project of a celebrated French modern architect, Chandigarh can, of course, easily be claimed for the West. Most of such claims consist of dismissing or eulogizing Chandigarh as an extension of Le Corbusier's œuvre, entirely disassociated from its Indian, third world, non-Western culture-scape. Based solely on superficial readings of form, the majority of scholarship on Chandigarh tends to scold Le Corbusier and the rest of the team of architects, along with the Indians who hired them, for callously importing a modernism from the West without thinking through its appropriateness for the Indian climes and contexts.[24] The only concession they generally offer is that Chandigarh's conception represents an attempt to overcome the sense of inferiority felt by the Nehruvian nation-state, which, coming straight out of colonization, advocated the unbridled imitation of the West. For them, Chandigarh was a mistake, a mask of shame.

While such readings are not entirely untrue, their perspective, I would argue, is much too one-dimensional. Chandigarh's modern architecture can of course be retraced to Western modern aesthetics, but in the 1980s scholars like Peter Serenyi and William J. R. Curtis have attempted to paint a fuller picture. In his book *Modern Architecture Since 1900*, Curtis derives the designs of Le Corbusier's Capitol from a culturally diverse palette of sources: the master plan from the Ville Radieuse, the Assembly plan from Schinkel's Altas Museum, and the Assembly portico from a building in the Mughal Red Fort of old Delhi, the "Diwan-i-Am."[25] According to Curtis, Le Corbusier's synthetic design-processes dissolved disparate temporal and spatial precedents into a unified whole:

> Indeed, the genesis of [Le Corbusier's] monumental vocabulary [in Chandigarh] seems to have involved a prodigious feat of abstraction in which devices from the Classical tradition— the grand order, the portico—were fused with Le Corbusier's generic system of forms in concrete (the "five points," the brise-soleil, etc.) and in turn cross-bred with Indian devices like the 'chattri', the trabeated terraces, balconies, and loggias of Fatehpur Sikri.[26]

The Symbolism of Chandigarh                    195

206  High Court,
Chandigarh, 1951–5.

207  Diwan-I-Am, Red
Fort, Delhi, early 17th
century.

208  Parliament (or
Assembly) Building,
Chandigarh, 1951–63.

**Fig. 1.6** Page 195 from Curtis 1986, illustrating the "Indianness" of the Capitol buildings.

Thus where other critics see a fundamental and unbridgeable schism between the East and the West, Curtis is able to ford it, by showing how differences are synthesized in the processes of design. Le Corbusier's "feat of abstraction," according to Curtis, "bridged the gap between East and West, ancient and modern, by seeking out correspondences in principle"[27] (fig 1.6).

Curtis, in fact, seems to make a special effort to exert the presence of Indianness in Le Corbusier's architecture, to the point that his arguments begin to seem fanciful. But the ultimate interests of Curtis's argument lie, of course, not in studying the architectural history of modern India—in the annals of which Chandigarh surely would be prominently mentioned—but in celebrating Le Corbusier. He is interested in making the case that it was Le Corbusier's exceptional synthetic capacity as a designer that was able to absorb and transform his Indian context into great architecture—"by seeking out correspondences in principle."

Whether one entirely agrees with his thesis or not, Curtis forces one to consider the proposition that, regardless of the immediate visual appearance of Le Corbusier's buildings, which seem entirely Western, the experience of being in India certainly must have made an impression on him—especially on a mind as synthetic as that of Le Corbusier. How could a historian detect perceptible traces of those impressions in the designs? It is this question that provided the initial impetus for my book, and to a good extent, chapters 3 and 4 still offer the fruits of that labor. These chapters are devoted to the analysis of Le Corbusier's ingestion of India into his aesthetic corpus, with all the discomforts and fascinations of that process.

My primary historiographical interests, however, do not lie in celebrating Le Corbusier. I explore his aesthetic process, his observations—along with those of Nehru, Fry, Drew, the administrators, and others involved in the capital project—to excavate the more hidden interests and desires underlying the making of Chandigarh. This book, therefore, is not devoted to the analysis of form for its own sake. Rather, it is an interpretation of form as cultural practice. Cultural studies that integrate formal analysis are fundamentally different from studies of form that refer to external cultural influences. For me, culture is always larger than any particular cultural practice—questions of aesthetics, spatial considerations, and the writing of architectural history, for instance, are always contained within and fundamentally defined by their larger cultural contexts. Thus, there is no such thing as pure art, or art for art's sake—that is merely a late nineteenth-century European idea. But the manner in which the larger institutions of culture define particular cultural practices is complex and diverse. There is no one way, or a preferred way, in which this process takes place. One can think of it in terms of the metaphor of theatrical "staging"—the stage on which, and the stage set within which, cultural practices like architectural aesthetics and historiography occur is that of the larger institution of culture.[28]

The case can be fleshed out by deconstructing Curtis's reading of Chandigarh. While Curtis's approach does challenge univalent representations of Chandigarh, the larger argument in which his discussion is couched remains trapped in a Eurocentric perspective. The Indian context and the question of an Indian perspective is negated, not by denying its presence but by making it subservient to Le Corbusier's personal design process. Curtis's argument relies on the assumption that a "prodigious feat of abstraction" enabled Le Corbusier to seek out "correspondences in principle" and to bridge the gap between identitarian and historical claims such as "East" and "West," "ancient" and "modern," in his aesthetic cauldron. But can abstraction, however prodigious, actually "bridge the gap" between the East and the West, the ancient and the modern? Is abstraction a universal solvent, a magical structure, a supra-neutral aesthetic process that lies above and beyond all historical and geographical claim?

It is not. Abstraction is a concept, an epistemic claim, which has its own history and specificity. It is an aesthetic concept claiming that the higher truths of the world immediately visible to us lie "behind" or "beyond" that world, in another more fundamental and unitary place of being. As such, it is also a moral assertion, since it entails the claim that the abstracted representation of the world is better, purer, and closer to some ultimate underlying truth that unifies all differences. One can trace the concept back to the parable of Plato's cave, where it is the invisible sun behind one's back that is the real truth that casts the shadows that one mistakes for reality. In the Judeo-Christian and Islamic theology abstraction is the fundamental nature of God, who is aniconic and unrepresentable. In modern abstract art it is the invisible underlying order of the visible world, now itself rendered visible and transparent.

It is no doubt a powerful concept. Yet, one can hardly doubt that it is nothing more than that—a concept, another representation of the world. The important point is that abstraction is a historical aesthetic device, a technique, a claim to seeing the world in a particular way, which has been privileged only in a particular cultural history and whose coherence stems only from its own particular genealogy.[29] Abstraction has been valued, especially in the West, because of its claim to represent the world neutrally, above and beyond the particularities of history and culture. But other cultures and other aesthetics make other claims. There are no aesthetic claims that are in fact universal and transhistorical. To present one's claims as such is always ideologically motivated.

In Curtis's argument, abstraction is presented as a universal and transhistorical feat.[30] My point in stating this is not to contest Le Corbusier's use of abstraction, nor the fact that abstraction is a powerful analytic and synthetic act. I will describe abstraction at work in Le Corbusier's aesthetic process as well.[31] When Curtis accepts and propagates abstraction as a universal act that supposedly does in fact dissolve historical and geographic differences—like those between the "East" and the "West"—his claim becomes Eurocentric since it does not historicize abstraction.

When one engages the task of representing an "Indian" or "non-Western" voice (as is the agenda of this book), one must thus account for the historical traffic of terms such as "East" and "West." Elaborated in the stories and reports of Western authors and administrators, such traffic has become known as orientalism; and orientalism was, as

Edward Said has demonstrated, not so much a figment of Western imagination as a systematic knowledge, assembled to describe the complexities and strangeness of the Orient within categories and comparisons that were coherent within Western epistemology.[32] As the opposite of the Westerners' own self-image, the Orient was perceived as feminine (exotic, mysterious, dark, and heavily ornamented), decrepit, static, tradition-bound, effete, and superficial. In this process, the Orient was produced not so much as the Occident's Other but as the Other within—a discourse of the Other, by, for, and of the West.[33]

Terms such as "Eastern," "vernacular," and "Indian" are thus implicated in a historically questionable legacy. In Curtis's narrative, abstraction does not dissolve the "East-West" opposition; rather it is an unguarded neo-oriental instance in which the "East" is negated and dissolved into the "West" and is irreparably "othered" and silenced in the process. It is an instance of what one could call epistemic colonization. Understanding historiography as epistemic colonization is not a simple matter of questioning Curtis's intentions; indeed, those are precisely to try to voice the non-West. Rather, it entails understanding the manner in which a historiographical method's own history must be accounted for. There are no universal epistemic claims.

And yet, if there is an ethical imperative at the heart of postcolonial historiography, it surely involves somehow voicing an authentic "non-West," beyond the stranglehold of "orientalism." This is the central postcolonial and deconstructive dilemma—i.e., how to work through, how to simultaneously inhabit and critique precisely what one is a part of, how to claim the mark of one's former master as one's own. To question the validity of modernism in the Third World from the point of view of universal claims versus local particularities is to reaffirm and reinstate a neo-colonial perspective from which modernism is recognizable only as the history of the expanding West.[34] This may be chronologically true. But chronology does not always explain history best. Although Chandigarh is an icon of modern architecture, it is, after all, in India and was built by and is occupied by Indians. How, then, can one rescue Chandigarh's history from Eurocentrism and rehabilitate it as Indian history—not just in its putatively "Indianized" elements, but in toto, with all its Western aesthetic?

Modern architecture has always and inevitably been considered a Western bequest, because its origins lie in Western history. Origins, however, are not ends, and therefore are not the only ways of deriving identity and ownership. There are other equally valid ways, such as adoption, participation, and appropriation. But origins are often presupposed to be the "natural" basis of identity. As a consequence, important histories of non-Western modernism, as non-originary claims, remain untold and misunderstood. These are my interests in this book—to claim and to explain Chandigarh's modernism not just as modern architecture, or modern Indian architecture, but as a non-originary Indian modern architecture. Adopted and appropriated by many, modern architecture, like all other cultural texts, belongs to the location where it is practiced, by Western or non-Western architects.

In other words, this book is a deconstruction of modernism, both as a Western and a non-Western construct. The important questions of historiography, I would argue, often do not lie in determining origins, but in assembling situational explanations, coherences whose validity can be judged within the context of their production, rather than against principles that are claimed to be foundational and universal. This is critical historiography—an assemblage of situational explanations, a textual strategy of reading.[35]

Understood as a cultural text, architecture has many existences in the differing social, cultural, and political perceptions of its authors, users, and interpreters. There is always something of a gap between the unconveyed aspirations and desires of the client, the secret inspirations and fascinations of the architect, and the distracted yet judgmental perceptions of the users. As such, an architectural construction is a multinucleated field, a complex mesh of signs, a creative document that simultaneously has an internal logic of its own and is created by and understood in the context in which it is situated.[36]

My historiographical method works with the active possibility that the various elements that went into the making of Chandigarh contested, contradicted, and even at times erased one another. What Nehru and the administrators of Punjab wanted, what Le Corbusier wanted to build and what he actually succeeded in having built, and what the inhabitants of Chandigarh understood they got, were distinct and different, even as they combined to produce the semblance of a singular event. The final design contained traces of the conflicts generated by the forces that went into its making.

Critical architectural historiography shifts the emphasis away from the intentions of the architect or the patron to a focus on the mechanics of the design. It concentrates on objects, rather than subjects, less on intention and more on meaning. It enables the historian to pose questions such as the ones raised by the "East-West" issue, without pretending to be recreating history "as it really happened" outside of authorial intervention. Regardless of whether or not Le Corbusier was able to "bridge the gap" between East and West, I ask, how is the binary "East-West" played out in the making of the city? How did Le Corbusier and Nehru internalize it? And then represent it?

In this book, I thus use Nehru and Le Corbusier's perspectives as highly charged condensations in order to precipitate larger political and cultural narratives. By examining the closely mirrored yet dramatically divergent investments of two of its prime movers, I narrate the story of Chandigarh, not as a simple effect of historical circumstances, but as a complex field of negotiated practices. In such a field, Chandigarh's characterization as a symbol of "modern India" is not a static and predetermined solvent that can be subjected to a litmus test of success or failure. Rather it is an open weave, a differentially shared, repeatedly negotiated, and unevenly contested terrain. Such a textual staging of contingent human practices, differentially inflected by political interests, I would argue, constitutes an ethical casting of historiography as postcolonial work. This opens possibilities of other narratives of the world, others than the ones cohered in univalent ideograms such as abstraction.

Similarly, my story is not for a single, but for multiple audiences in history and theory. As a historical study it is for the students and scholars of modern architecture in general and for students of modern South Asian history in particular. Given its more theoretical imperatives it is also addressed to those in indisciplinary fields, such as cultural studies and postcolonial studies.

At the same time, I would venture that the book is also accessible and available to nonspecialists. It is written in a somewhat novelistic manner with preludes and leading questions. Wherever I have felt it necessary to engage a larger theoretical debate, I have tried to keep the language as simple as possible, while maintaining specificity of meaning. Hence, I believe that this book will appeal to the general reader, not only because it is autobiographical but also because the actual imagined audience with whom I was "speaking" in my mind's eye while writing consisted, in fact, not of trained scholars of postcoloniality but of the students of the Chandigarh College of Architecture. Not that different from those in other schools of architecture, these students still carry the weight of a sense of a "grand" legacy—Chandigarh, Le Corbusier—and wrestle to define their own identity with respect to that, in spite of it. For them this book is intended to answer some questions, mostly historical, and raise some others, generally theoretical.

I have chosen my representative audience, not only because I can claim to belong to it, but more so because it offers a perspective that is interested equally in Le Corbusier's "Western" modernism and in India and its social, cultural, and political circumstances and desires. In the postcolonial world, to be interested in the institutions of the West, especially as they were practiced in the non-West, is to be interested in the interests of the non-West.

Take the everyday phrase "modern-Indian": in Nehruvian India, the "East-West" opposition was translated into the binary "modern-Indian." This is still the case—everything must be simultaneously "modern" and "Indian." This is, for one, a Hegelian view of history, in which progress always occurs through the transformative overcoming of oppositions. If one accepts it as such, the binary "modern-Indian" offers the historian a quick test to evaluate success or failure—Chandigarh's architecture either did or did not successfully synthesize and overcome the opposition.

But what is "Indian" and what is "modern"? And must modernity and Indianness necessarily be exclusive of each other? In the specifics of the Indian cultural context, the term "modern-Indian" is doubly problematic. First, the word "modern" in India today not only implies something "contemporary," it also implies Western, superior, and better. Thus, while the emergence into modernity is accepted in the West as part of the continuing devolution of its own history, in postcolonial India, modernity inevitably signifies a break with its own history and the superiority of the West. To be modern in India today is to acknowledge the presence of the West, of the outsider that is of necessity inside—for reasons of "progress." It signifies, in other words, an outsider-inside.

Second, the term "Indian" is even more problematic. It derives from a historical account. When approached from the west, India lies across the river Indus; the term

Indian thus refers to the land across the Indus. "India" therefore makes sense, quite literally, only from the historical, western perspective. In precolonial times, the term "India," like the term "Europe," was useful only as a sign that distinguished it from that which was "not India." Within "India," as within "Europe," there were innumerable kingdoms and principalities that constantly and fervently distinguished themselves from one another.

Today "India" also refers, of course, to the nation-state, which is equally a modern, Western concept, brought across the Indus, one among many. "Indian" thus is a concept and signifier that is Western in origin. Like "modern," the term "Indian" in India today should also signify an outsideness-inside. But in this case, its outsideness is repressed and camouflaged. This repression, however, enables one to signify and claim the "truly Indian," even if hidden in scare-quotes.[37]

This camouflaged collusion of the "modern" and the "Indian," this condition in which hierarchical binaries such as "Indian" and "modern," "vernacular" and "contemporary," "East" and "West," "past" and "present," etc., are persistently linked on the basis of their difference and persist in the name of a certain ideal of progress whose referential center always resides in a mythological West, is the description of the postcolonial condition. This is modern India, the nature of the Indian modernity. With subtle subterfuge, the "Orient" today lives in the wake of its colonial past.[38] The "post" in postcolonial is descriptive of that identity and agency that comes to life both as the end of the colonial and also as its inheritance.

This is how I propose the following book, as the story of the making of a "modern-Indian" event, of an "East-West" encounter presented as that of the formation of an Indian modern architecture. The writing of this book also participates in this process. Salman Rushdie, writing his own brand of Hindi-English, or Hinglish, as he calls it, appropriates English for himself as a postcolonial writer. His writing is not derivative, his idiom is his own. Postcolonial histories and practices of modernisms, in the same way, need not apologize for their modernity. One does not need to "Indianize" them; they were/are Indian always.

## Chapters of the Book

At one level, the book follows a simple hierarchical order, diminishing in scale by chapters. It begins with the design of the overall Master Plan for the city (1950). This account is followed by two chapters on Le Corbusier's design of the main Capitol Complex—the governmental center with the State High Court, Legislative Assembly, and Secretariat (1950–60); and the book finishes with a discussion of the city's emblem, the Open Hand (1955–84). As such, this book can be read as a roughly chronological account of the history of the making of Chandigarh.

At another level, however, the book unfolds in response to a series of instigating questions. Each chapter occupies an investigative world of its own and offers a conclusion to an outstanding issue from the past. Together they can be read as narrating a series of quests, both political and aesthetic.

Chapter 2 engages the question of Chandigarh's modernism. Who really determined the urban character of Chandigarh? While there was never any doubt that Chandigarh was to be a "modern" city, what kind of modernity was appropriate for Chandigarh remained open to question and, given the city's symbolic importance, was hotly contested. Nehru, Le Corbusier, and the city administrators all had differing conceptions of the modern, and their confrontation describes some of the competing interests of the newly independent Indian nation-state. Shuttling between the winning and losing voices of this struggle, this chapter tells the tale of the mirrored misrecognitions that set the stage for Chandigarh's development.

Chapter 3 undertakes an interpretation of the Capitol Complex. What is the symbolic subtext of Le Corbusier's cryptic and colossal Capitol Complex? In reconstructing the cultural moorings of this idealized landscape, this chapter is motivated by the search not for Le Corbusier's formal design precedents, but for his perception and representation of India. Le Corbusier's representation of the ambitions of the new nation-state, veiled and romanticized as it is, is of fundamental epistemic value to the primary inheritors of Chandigarh, i.e., its residents and the second generation of Indian modern architects. India's tryst with an imported modernism is a legacy that the current generation is still working through and overcoming. Addressed to this generation, this chapter uncovers the apocalyptic yet sadly naïve underpinnings of Le Corbusier's heroics, in order to demystify and humanize a fallen hero and a failed promise of deliverance.

Chapter 4 constitutes a psychoanalytic reading of the Capitol buildings. What is the buildings' aesthetic value? Continuing from chapter 3, this chapter engages in a reading of the aesthetic construction of the High Court and the Assembly. Using concepts drawn from Freudian psychoanalysis, these readings suggest ways in which memories from Le Corbusier's distant past, along with the impressions of his tenure in India, were woven into his aesthetic compositions of the Capitol buildings. The aesthetic "brilliance" of these buildings is generally unquestioned in the canon of modern architecture. They are considered the tour de force of Le Corbusier's late œuvre. In playful dialogue with this canon, my interpretations are offered as contextual explanation of their aesthetics, not to glorify or ridicule the architect but to liberate one's self from their uncanny aesthetic suggestions—and to laugh at the ironic perversion of their compositions.

Chapter 5 offers three interpretations of the Open Hand. What is the meaning of the Open Hand and why was it constructed only in the 1980s, and not with the rest of the Capitol? The Open Hand is one of the most recognized of Le Corbusier's creations. It is the official emblem not only of the city of Chandigarh but also of the foundation dedicated to the preservation and propagation of Le Corbusier's archives. Building on the syntax of the previous chapters, this chapter offers three disparate readings of the Open Hand, which demonstrate the Hand's inherent and natural multivalence. As the readings miss each other, they also tell the story of a series of political misrepresentations and misunderstandings, in character with the story of Chandigarh as I have narrated it.

Thus, chapters 2 and 5 form the more political of the readings, while chapters 3 and 4 constitute the more aesthetic ones. In these couplings, then, lies another way to read this book.

Most of my material has been drawn from Le Corbusier's fragmented and disconnected sketchbooks. Loose and unstructured as they are, they furnish a mine of information and questions. They are unformalized memoirs, whose information ranges from a reminder to buy a hula hoop to "fight the encroaching belly" (4#294), to job lists, and speculations on the human condition. I have concentrated on the sketchbooks that are associated with each of Le Corbusier's visits to India, and have used the translations provided in the Notes published with them. The drawings I use are those that are published in the *Œuvre complète* or in the *Le Corbusier Archives*.[39] Supplemental drawings and correspondence were found in the Fondation Le Corbusier (FLC) in Paris, and the archives of the Capitol Project at the Chandigarh Museum, Chandigarh.

*Each chapter begins with a gestural prologue written in the first person. That voice, for me, represents my commitment to you, the reader.*

# Contesting Conceptions
# of the Modern

While Chandigarh was being constructed and long after it was done, numerous Indian celebrities passed though our house—Mulk Raj Anand, the first Indian novelist published in English, Prithviraj Kapoor, the grandfather of Indian cinema, Zul Vellani, actor and commentator, Charles Correa and Balkrishna Doshi, the rising young stars of Indian modern architecture, and others—all of whom were there to make their regular pilgrimage to the new capital. And then there was the stream of Western architects and intellectuals, most of whom, besides William Curtis, I barely remember. But I do remember that my father would force these unsuspecting visitors to sit through hours of readings from his innumerable book manuscripts, hurling challenges at them across the smoky drawing room to dispute his arguments. His manuscripts were in free verse and afforded a high degree of interpretation. A counter-claim followed every claim. Words were not minced.

These embarrassing occasions were amongst the many ways in which I put together my early mythologized memory of the meaning of Chandigarh. As scotch and soda flowed, and while my mother, Savitri Prakash (née Gupta), cooked patiently in the kitchen, my sisters and I watched with wondrous eyes as accusations and denunciations flew across the room, and Nehru, Le Corbusier, and the whole gamut of modern architecture were made easy cannon fodder. At that time, little did we realize that what we were silent witnesses to was less an intellectual debate and more an anxiety play, the travails of a generation wrestling with the true legacy of its creations.

To claim his stake in the legacy, my father did publish two books—*Chandigarh: A Presentation in Free Verse* (1978) and *Reflections on Chandigarh* (1983). The writing of this book, thus, is not only an act of retracing my own identity as shaped by my birthplace, but indeed also that of my father. Bowing to the exigencies of patriarchy, the thesis on which this book is based was dedicated:

> To my father, Aditya Prakash, who,
> even as he helped give birth to, was born of Chandigarh.

Claiming birth through that which you helped midwife is a narcissistic act that denies the necessity of parentage, of an incipient legacy. It is like renaming oneself as an adult, as Le Corbusier did, as if one could do away with one's paternity by recreating oneself. It is something of a monstrosity, pregnant with utopian promise, driven by the fear of failure. But for Nehru's midnight children the 1950s were a heady time, and claiming new births, at whatever price, was the name of the game.

While those drawing room debates continued well into the night, my mother always preferred to head to bed right after dinner. She had come to Chandigarh as a young bride, when the city was but a handful of tents. She had watched it grow, and now, as she once told me, "not much could be done about it." I wondered what she meant.

My father wrote that the making of Chandigarh was "like the rising of the Phoenix from the ashes of its own fire." It was meant, he noted, "to restore a meaning to life." What meaning did Chandigarh restore to life? Fathered by Jawaharlal Nehru, Chandigarh, as Charles Correa put it, was born "without umbilical cord, in the harsh plains of Punjab."[1] Without umbilical cord, Chandigarh was supposedly conceived with no preconceptions; it was, in other words, a "modern" city. What is the meaning of restoring life by claiming birth "without umbilical cord"? What is it to be "modern"? How were such things claimed?

While we were growing up in Chandigarh, the city's modernness made us feel simultaneously privileged and denied. Modernity, associated with ideas of progress and development, is always at a premium in the third world. At the same time it is a curse. For every time we went out of Chandigarh, met other architects and architecture students, we were always told how Chandigarh was not "Indian," and therefore a failure. The only major book on Chandigarh, an old thesis of Norma Evenson's from the early 1960s, repeated the same diagnosis. By the late 1970s, all the institutions of modernism were under fire around the world, and questions of history, regional identity, and difference were in vogue. Postmodernism was in anticipation, and being modern, a.k.a. not being properly Indian, hung like the albatross around one's neck.

*Most of what matters in our lives takes place in our absence.*
*—Salman Rushdie,* Midnight's Children

*At this moment the child is made, he is born. The decision is irrevocable. Its appearance? Its beauty? Everything depends on the choice that was made, which resides in its constituents and in the variations arising from their combination. Consequently the resulting form; its character is but one among a thousand other possibilities. Before us every possibility is waiting …*
*—Le Corbusier,* Le Poème de l'angle droit

One of the most significant and overwhelming characteristics of Chandigarh is that it is not a visibly "Indian" city. One feels this everywhere, in the streets that lack the "Indian" intimacy in their scale, in the details of the architecture that is stark and clean, and most of all in the urban order that is rectilinear, neatly organized by sectors and house numbers. Traffic flows in an orderly pattern and there are no wandering cows. All the shops are defined by "frame control"—no profuse ornamentation, identical heights, similar windows. And most of the houses in the city, both those built by the state and those privately developed, follow strict, minimalist rhythms.

In postcolonial India, "Indian" and "modern" are considered to be opposites and exclusive of each other. Chandigarh is considered to be "un-Indian" simply because it is self-consciously constructed as a "modern" city. Modernity is not, of course, the exclusive preserve of the West, but it is a legacy of the colonial distribution of the western epistemic universe that only things that are precolonial are considered "Indian." This not only forestalled India's autonomous advent into modernity, but also made anything that was modern in India into something that was Western.

Such binary thinking tends to crystallize perceptions into black and white. The vivid perception of Chandigarh's lack of Indianness provokes the reciprocal assumption that its modernness must be similarly transparent and univalent. When one examines the record, however, one finds that ideas of what was "modern" and how "modern" was "modern" enough *were* open to question and hotly contested. The contestants were many: Nehru's conception of the modern at times coincided with those of Le Corbusier and at other times not; Le Corbusier himself was at loggerheads with the other western architects of the project; and in the midst of it all, the administrative officials of the government of Punjab, the official clients and executors of the project, nurtured their own conception of the modern, which, with the authority of government passing through their pens, was more often than not the final word.[2]

In this chapter, I retrace the competing manifestations of the modern that gave expression to Chandigarh's fundamental urban and architectural character. I emphasize the competitive nature of the claims to Chandigarh's fabled modernity, not only to challenge the supposed transparence of the claim, but also to flesh out some of the meanings of the "modern" in the postcolonial world. As the various viewpoints challenged and contested each other, alliances were formed that tell as much about the fractures and fissures of the congealing polity of the new Indian nation-state, as of varying understandings of modernity and modern architecture.

## Early Decisions: A. L. Fletcher vs. P. L. Verma

The person who emerged as the first claimant to Chandigarh's modernity was a senior Indian bureaucrat, A. L. Fletcher, "Officer on Special Duty" to the government of Punjab assigned solely to deal with the New Capital. A product of the erstwhile British Civil Service, Fletcher belonged to that cadre of civil servants who took over and essentially continued colonial administrative practices. As a bureaucrat, Fletcher's role was technically only advisory; nevertheless he seemed to have clearly been the man in charge, much more so than the elected officials. Most of his long memos to the government received brief replies, and the agenda and propositions he put forth generally returned from the cabinet unaltered, with the stamp of approval. Some of the Punjab cabinet's early lack of active involvement in specific design decisions concerning the New Capital project might be explained by the fact that the state's government was beset with a slew of political problems at the time.[3] But it seems equally plausible that the demanding expectations of the Nehruvian modernity constantly required "new and good" proposals, the generation of which became the lot of the bureaucrats, who, unlike the newly elected political representatives, were viewed to be well-versed in modern Western thinking.

Consequently, Fletcher clearly thought that it was his duty and prerogative to research and advocate what the character of the New Capital should be. By May 1948, just a few months after his appointment, Fletcher had already prepared a detailed "Note on the New Capital" for the consideration of the Punjab cabinet. Fletcher was meticulous and well organized, and his preparatory notes, still available in the Chandigarh Museum Archives, tell his story well.

Fletcher's notes begin, appropriately enough, with a collection of questionnaires. The neatly typed index announces that these were for the "High Court," the "University," the "Education Department," on "Health and Medical," on "Social Life and Recreation," and on "Industry," "Trading Facilities," and "Commerce." Initially, the questions appear logical and innocent enough. They seem to be aimed at defining logistical parameters such as the quantity and character of the court rooms, the suitability of air-conditioning, the necessity of accompanying hostels, expected occupancy, desired recreational facilities and residential communities, maximum travel distances, the types of hospitals needed, etc.

A more careful reading, however, reveals a different picture. Fletcher's true questions in fact are only limited to the more rudimentary programmatic concerns that are likely to have actual spatial and infrastructural requirements that he cannot anticipate. For the larger issues pertaining to policy, Fletcher strongly "suggests" the appropriate answer with leading questions. For instance, question 3 under "Education" states:

> The Sargent Plan which is very ably considered in the "Plan for Education by F. G. Pearce, Oxford University Press" has valuable suggestions to make regarding the types of schools. Do you think that the recommendations made in the Sargent Plan could be made the basis of our educational institutions?[4]

As one continues through the file, it emerges that the so-called questionnaires on "Social Life" and "Industry" do not have any questions at all, but are in fact manifestos. Thus, the "questionnaire" of "Social Life and Recreation in Our New Capital" begins by noting that "it is not possible, and even if it were it would not be wise, to prescribe the social and cultural pattern of a new town. The interest, groupings and cultural activities of citizens must grow of themselves." Nevertheless, Fletcher goes on to state that "there are, however, certain facilities that are found in most towns and we should therefore make similar provisions."[5]

Fletcher's list of those certain facilities "found in most towns" contains "Theatre, Music and the Arts," "Libraries," "Archives and Museum," "Places of Refreshment and Hotels," "Registered Clubs," "Space for Recreation," "Parks, Public Gardens and Playing Fields," "Special Needs of Young People," and "Spectator Sports." Similarly, Fletcher's questionnaire on "Industry" begins by noting the economic circumstances that are likely to determine growth of industry, but then goes on to prescribe a series of constraints and proscriptions that should determine the locations of industry in the New Capital.

Where did Fletcher derive his answers to these pseudo-questionnaires? As one reads on, it becomes evident that Fletcher researched contemporary town planning methods in the West, and, based on these, developed his agendas for the New Capital. This is not how he explicitly presents his argument, but his intentions are clear enough for his hand to be forced in July 1948 by P. L. Verma, the chief engineer of the Public Works Department, the agency responsible for the construction of the future city. Instead of researching contemporary town planning, Verma proposes, there should be a limited international competition for the design of Chandigarh. Verma argues that since the contemporary conditions of India are unique and unusual, it would be best to float a competition that could generate the best ideas.[6]

Fletcher totally disagrees with Verma's idea and makes a strong case against it.[7] In his "Note on the Competition Idea Sponsored by C. E. (Dev.),"[8] Fletcher argues that the proposal was "intrinsically unsound" and would require excessive government expenditure. "Planning a New Capital," he protests, "is not like planning for a hospital, or a school, or even a housing scheme. … It is a complicated process that"—and here he quotes Sir Patrick Abercrombie, Chairman of the English New Towns Committee of 1946—"must be looked upon as 'an essay in civilization.' … That is why town and country planning eminently calls for the services of a particular kind of expert planner, of whom Professor Abercrombie is at present the outstanding example. … The idea of a competition is suitable for enterprises of a limited scope," he concludes, "whereas, for planning a new town—an enterprise covering the whole gamut of human relations and activities—the idea is open to grave objections."[9]

"We must," Fletcher instead proposes, "be guided by the views of those who have had such experience [with the building of new towns], and follow the practice evolved in countries that have built or are building new towns":

> F. J. Osborne … has been actively associated with the building of two new towns and who was a member of the New Towns Committee set up in England in 1946 [which] are Letchworth and Welwyn in England. Most of what I have to say is based on a study of his book "Green Belt Cities." … Osborn is thus an acknowledged authority on the subject. So are Louis [sic] Mumford (American), G. D. H. Cole (English), Sir Ebenezer Howard (English) (Originator of Garden City idea and author of the book 'Garden Cities of Tomorrow'), E. A. Gutkin [sic], author of 'Creative Demobilization (2 volumes),' R. E. Dickinson, author of 'City Region and Regionalism' and Professor Sir Patrick Abercrombie

who is universally acclaimed as one of the greatest practicing authorities on the subject and is the author of many classic plans such as the Greater London Plan, 1944.[10]

"The views that I am advancing in this note are based on a comparative study of these authorities," Fletcher concludes, "[and] not one of them has a word to say about the competition idea."

Although he makes it sound as if they had been building towns for a long time, Fletcher's "authorities" were in fact part of the avant-garde of new town planning thinking in the West—the Garden City movement, whose fundamental goal was to invent new living environments that could coexist with heavy industry without suffering from the congestion and squalor that resulted from industrial pollution and the agglomeration of labor. Its origins lie in the late nineteenth-century social critiques of industrialization. In 1898, English social theorist Ebenezer Howard published *To-Morrow: A Peaceful Path to Real Reform,*[11] in which he advocated the creation of new towns of limited size that were surrounded by a permanent belt of agricultural land. He argued that town and country were the two magnets of modern life and proposed a "town-country" balance to benefit from both. To maintain this balance, he insisted on segregating functions in the city. In his book, he published a diagram modeling his ideal garden city, which consists of a large round central park, surrounded by concentric rings of houses and gardens, a grand avenue and secondary streets, while all the factories are located in the outermost rings, which are connected by railway. Beyond these rings there is only the permanent agricultural belt consisting of farmlands. The whole idea depended on there being well-defined limits to the size of new towns to prevent congestion and to maintain active contact with the farmlands. Howard proposed a cap of 30,000 residents.[12]

Howard's book was republished in 1902 as the *Garden Cities of To-Morrow*. This edition became famous, and the Garden City principles were adopted in two model developments, Letchworth (1903) and Welwyn (1919) in England, and in Radburn, New Jersey (1929) in the United States. Howard's emphasis on a permanent agricultural zone around towns was eventually adopted by British planners with its most impressive application in the 1944 plan for Greater London, developed by Sir Patrick Abercrombie. After the passage of the New Towns Act of 1946, Howard's ideas were actively deployed to develop a ring of new towns around London and eventually became institutionalized as planning dogma.

Based on these ideas, Fletcher proposed a vision for Chandigarh that ultimately determined the basic character of the city. Specifically, Fletcher proposed that the New Capital should consist of three small towns, or "units," to limit growth and ensure access to agricultural land. These units were an Administrative Center, a University Township, and a Satellite Industrial Town. He expected the primary center, the administrative unit, to develop to a population of 100,000. No industry was to be located here except "service industries such as laundries, bakeries, etc." Although the exact location of the University Township had not been decided, Fletcher noted that it should be as far as possible from the Administrative Center, but within the fifty square miles site that had been approved for the New Capital. The third unit, the Satellite Industrial Town, was to be built explicitly on the Garden City principles, to accommodate all except "heavy and obnoxious industries." Fletcher did not, however, describe the location of this unit.

Fletcher expected the three units to function as a single city because he expected "motorized transport" to carry the residents from one unit to another. Predicated on the presumed success of the car, Fletcher's argument was developed in his memo as a paean to modernity:

> The modern metropolitan community, unlike the pre-motor city, obtains its unity through territorial differentiation of specialized functions rather than through mass participation in centrally located institutions. … The modern city is consequently no longer a compact settlement unit. It is becoming the headquarters of a group of interrelated towns and satellite settlements which yet form one community centred upon the city. This specialization of function associated with the close interrelations of widely scattered places to form an integrated functional unit with subordinate centres in the towns but with the nerve centre in the city, is the essential characteristic of modern society in civilized lands.[13]

That India had only just started large-scale industrialization and that the "motor city" was still a long way off was, of course, not taken into account by Fletcher. He did not even consider alternative, say indigenous, ways of inventing the New Capital. Instead, he advocated his vision as a "modern" idea, which he knew was the currency of the Nehruvian state and the mandate of Chandigarh.

In 1948, when Fletcher was extensively quoting all its protagonists, the Garden City concept was a radical new idea that had recently been adopted by the English planning institutions to rebuild their postwar cities. What is curious about Fletcher's arguments, however, is that he never foregrounds the relatively radical character of the Garden City movement and is, in fact, at pains to point out that this was the gospel of all new towns developed by the "authorities." There were many other interrelated utopian city ideas in circulation in Europe and the United States at the time—such as Tony Garnier's Cité Industrielle (1917), Le Corbusier's Ville Contemporaine (1922) and Ville Radieuse (c.1930), and Frank Lloyd Wright's Broadacre City (1936)—but Fletcher does not even refer to any of them, indicating his preference for ideas that could be presented as institutionalized by the English. He constantly mentions Letchworth and Welwyn as examples of new towns developed according to the Garden City principles, but never notes that these were among the very few towns built experimentally according to those principles. He strives instead to establish a natural and easy continuum between the publishing of Howard's book and the New Towns Act of 1946. Of a no doubt well-entrenched neocolonial mindset, Fletcher must have grappled with the challenges to authority and tradition that Nehru's new and modern modernity posed. Discovering an idea that was both modern and yet institutionalized in the West must have seemed ideal to him.

On the "authority" of his sources, Fletcher was able to successfully oppose Verma's competition idea. On 30 August 1948, Fletcher issued a press statement announcing "important decisions" taken by the cabinet subcommittee for the New Capital in a meeting held two days prior. There is little difference between Fletcher's recommendations and the cabinet's decisions. The cabinet approved that the New Capital would be planned in the three units. Fletcher also noted that Verma would be

> going to the United Kingdom and the United States of America within about a month for the final selection of our Town Planner, Chief Architect and Architects. The Chief Secretary to Government, East Punjab, has already written to our embassies of these countries for the engagement of these experts and our Chief Engineer will proceed to these countries as soon as the negotiations are in the final stage. A number of other experts will also have to be engaged at a later stage. Experts for air-conditioning, lighting, traffic and landscape artists are included in this category.[14]

P. L. Verma, however, continued steadfastly through the year 1949 to oppose Fletcher's idea to develop Chandigarh on the principle of three separate units. Verma contended that Fletcher's analysis relied on English history and social practices that were not applicable to India. While Verma did not argue against the basic principles of the Garden City movement, he thoroughly disagreed with Fletcher on the expectations of growth for Chandigarh. Fletcher felt that there would not be demand for more than 150,000–200,000 inhabitants and therefore was sure that his administrative and university units could accommodate them. For Fletcher, industry could be absorbed either in existing cities or in newly developed industrial areas adjacent to existing ones. Verma on the contrary argued for a single large town with an ultimate expected population of 500,000, claiming that besides the necessary administrative and university functions, Chandigarh would also be settled by the massive business community that had been displaced from Pakistan. New industry, according to Verma, should also be located within Chandigarh to stimulate economic growth.[15]

In sum, Verma argued that Chandigarh should be envisioned as a more typical city with integrated multiple functions while preserving modern Garden City ideals, whereas Fletcher wanted Chandigarh to be a more utopian city based on idealized expectations. On 30 November 1948, Fletcher wrote another note pleading his case. "I have consistently maintained," Fletcher advocated,

> that an architect should be the presiding genius in the planning of the town. The latest cable from our High Commissioner in the United Kingdom is in support of my view. I would, therefore, advise the Government that the question of the technical men required for the planning of our Capital should be entrusted to the President of [the] Royal Institute of British Architects and we should accept his advice in the matter. We should not in a matter of such supreme importance be influenced by local or departmental considerations.[16]

Eventually, however, the differences between them came to a head and Verma forced the chief minister to choose between them. The government's decision came down in his favor, and Fletcher was removed from the job. Thus Verma's vision for the New Capital prevailed, and Chandigarh was developed as a single unit.

Today, in public opinion, usually only Verma is credited for forging the basic vision of the city, and Fletcher is all but forgotten. Nevertheless, it is important to remember that it was Fletcher's first decision to cast Chandigarh in a Garden City mold that always held sway, while all later attempts to rethink the fundamental character of the city were thwarted. As modern and radical as Chandigarh was, its own incumbency quickly became dogma.

## First Plan: Albert Mayer and Matthew Nowicki

Late in 1949, preparations were finally made for Verma to travel to England to recruit the town planners and architects. Nehru, however, torpedoed the whole plan. When permission was sought from him to send Verma abroad, Nehru opposed the idea politely, but vehemently. "I do not wish to come in your way in this matter," Nehru wrote back, "but I wonder if you have explored the possibilities of getting the master plan made in India … there is too great a tendency for our people to rush up to England and America for advice. The average American or English town-planner will probably not know the social background of India. He will therefore be inclined to plan something which might suit England or America, but not so much India."[17]

On 11 December 1949, Gopi Chand Bhargav, the Chief Minister of Punjab, wrote a short note to Fletcher and Verma, concurring with Nehru that a "Town Planner from abroad will not know the conditions in India." Instead, he suggested that Albert Mayer, an American town planner who was working in the state of Uttar Pradesh at that time, be interviewed for the job.[18] The selection of Mayer offered a happy compromise. In him the government of Punjab would have someone who not only had the high level of training and expertise that the job required, and which no Indian planner had, but who also had years of experience in India and therefore was very familiar with Indian conditions and requirements. That is how Verma and P. N. Thapar, the new financial commissioner of Punjab, came to meet Mayer in New Delhi on 20 December 1949 and subsequently hired him, after obtaining approval from the government of Punjab.[19]

Albert Mayer (1897–1983) started out as a civil engineer with a degree from the Massachusetts Institute of Technology (1919). Later he became a licensed architect and founded the New York architectural firm of Mayer and Whittlesey, essentially devoted to large-scale housing studies. In the 1930s he became very active in Franklin D. Roosevelt's New Deal to prepare a new federal housing policy, and in collaboration with urban historians and theorists Lewis Mumford and Henry Wright, he founded a housing research group called the Housing Study Guild, which lasted for about five years.[20]

World War II took Mayer to India as an Army engineer to build airfields in Bengal for the China-Burma-India theater. During his stay he became very interested in Indian rural life and in 1945 seized the opportunity of a chance introduction to Jawaharlal Nehru to propose building model villages to stimulate economic and social progress. On 1 May 1946, on the eve of independence, Nehru invited Mayer to return to India as advisor to the government of the state of Uttar Pradesh on "various matters related to planning, village reconstruction and the ordered development of community life more especially in our rural areas."[21]

In the fall of 1946, Mayer took an exploratory trip through rural Uttar Pradesh and this experience convinced him that, as Robert Emmett reports,

> the social economic base for self-sustaining development did not yet exist. Mayer had seen that the earlier developmental efforts of the government, missionaries, and Gandhian "constructive workers" had failed when outside supports were removed. He therefore dropped his initial suggestion of a program to build model villages, proposing instead to organize an integrated rural development program. Mayer saw the benefits of increased agricultural production not as ends in themselves, but as means of raising the level of village expectation and stimulating a self-sustaining participation in local development.[22]

Immediately after 15 August 1947, Nehru appointed Mayer as the "Planning Advisor to the Government of Uttar Pradesh." Mayer immediately started work on the pilot rural development project, which subsequently became famous as the Etawah Project (named for the district where it was begun). The project was based on the principle of what Mayer called "inner democratization," a process foreshadowing the working method of some of the Indian non-governmental organizations (NGOs) that developed later. The core of the inner democratization process was the "Village Level Worker," usually a member of the village itself, who was to act as a liaison between the village and the government, who had the confidence of the former and the ear of the latter, and who, unlike an appointed official, was personally invested in the development of the district which she or he represented. Other innovations of the Etawah Project included a rural newspaper to bring farmers abreast with modern agricultural techniques and the appointment of the "Rural Life Analyst," an anthropologist who was "a detached social-technical observer capable of quickly anticipating and communicating village reactions in order to facilitate the early correction of misjudgments."[23]

At the same time Mayer was also involved in some urban planning projects. In 1947, he was appointed as a consultant to Greater Bombay (now Mumbai). Working with the municipal engineer of Bombay, N. V. Modak, Mayer prepared two study master plans for Greater Bombay. The Modak-Mayer plan suggested the extension of the Bombay municipality further north to Vashi and proposed new north-south expressways, as well as the idea of developing the land across the bay (now New Mumbai).[24]

When he was appointed to prepare the Master Plan of Chandigarh, Mayer thus was well entrenched in India and had been addressing issues of development with an aggressive and innovative mindset. He was clearly very sympathetic to the needs and expectations of the Indian way of life, but, building on his experiences working on Roosevelt's New Deal projects, Mayer was also committed to the processes of state-sponsored modernization. These two ideals were, of course, also those of Jawaharlal Nehru, and the two as a consequence maintained close contact through correspondence.

After accepting the Chandigarh commission, Mayer, in a letter to Nehru dated 1 May 1950, reported on the progress he had made:

> I am thrilled at the [Master Plan]. I feel in all solemnity that this will be a source of great stimulation of city building and re-planning in India. But I also feel that it will be the most complete synthesis and integration in the world to date of all that has been learned and talked of in planning over the last 30 years, but which no one has yet had the great luck to be allowed actually to create. Yet I feel we have been able to make it strongly Indian in feeling and function, as well as modern.[25]

**Fig. 2.1** Albert Mayer's master plan. (Chandigarh Museum Archives)

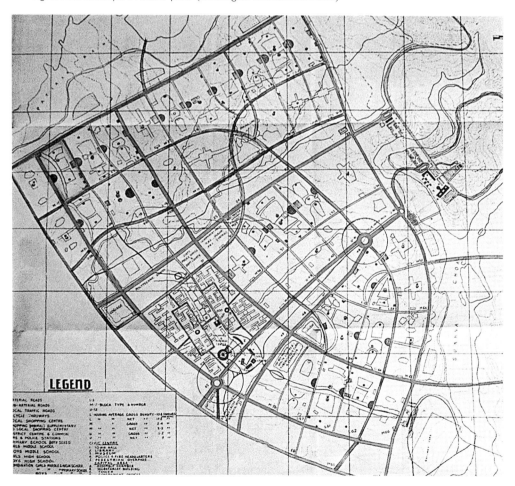

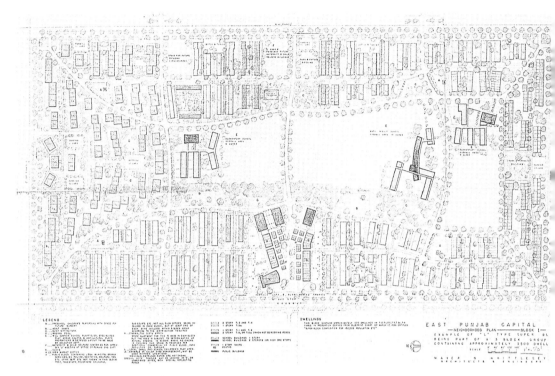

**Fig. 2.2** Superblock design by Albert Mayer.

"Strongly Indian in feel and function, as well as modern," Mayer's master plan was based on all the basic principles of the Garden City movement. His fan-shaped plan organized the city into residential neighborhoods of 1350 x 900 meters called "superblocks," that were further subdivided into three equal blocks. Each superblock accommodated the basic amenities of a neighborhood such as a market, primary and secondary schools, hospital, meeting hall, etc. The entire city was organized by a vehicular circulation system with the roads curved to respond to the natural features of the terrain.[26] The administrative capitol was located at the very north in the middle of a lake and the commercial complex dominated the middle (figs. 2.1, 2.2).

The "Indianness" to which Mayer referred lay in the decorative treatment of the surfaces and the undulations of the skyline. There is also a sense that the internal streets may have contained some roadside kiosks and place for other activities, abstracted from the Indian bazaars.[27] Mayer contracted Polish-born American architect Matthew Nowicki (b. 1910) to visualize the architecture. Nowicki's sketches show intimate urban environments that have a vague "Indian" feel to them, consisting essentially of stylized animal motifs on the walls, abstracted temple designs, and a house with an internal courtyard (plate 3).

However, one will never know how fully "Indian in feeling and function" Mayer-Nowicki's design might eventually have been, because Nowicki died in an airplane crash over Egypt on 31 August 1950. Mayer could conceivably have continued the work with a new architect, but the government officers of Punjab seized the opportunity to reassert the case that they had to undertake an extensive journey to Europe to find a new team of architects and town planners. Nehru again objected: "I do not understand how a person touring Europe and America, stopping for a few days at each place, can help in [the capital project]. It may be good for the persons concerned from an educational point of view. Specially at this time of acute financial stringency any expenditure that is not absolutely essential might be avoided."[28] But this time the bureaucracy prevailed, and in November 1950 the new administrative head of the capital project, P. N. Thapar, and P. L. Verma were sent on a month-long voyage to select suitable replacements.

## Second Plan: Le Corbusier at Work

Initially, Thapar and Verma approached Maxwell Fry and Jane Drew, an English husband/wife architect team that had been doing work abroad. They certainly had the right experience, as Maxwell Fry's curriculum vitae reported:

> My partner and I are architects to the Gold Coast Government for programmes of school and hospital building, for the development work in the Gambia, and for the building of the new Nigerian University at Ibadan. We are architects to the Kuwait on the Persian Gulf, work for which is nearly completed. As Advisors to the Resident Minister (1944–46) we made Master Plans for many towns and regions in West African Colonies, and drew up draft Town Planning legislation which has since passed into law.[29]

However, since Fry and Drew had older commitments, the two agreed to work only on the housing and recommended instead that Le Corbusier be employed for the Master Plan and the Capitol buildings. Although initially Le Corbusier seemed reluctant, he soon changed his mind on the condition that Pierre Jeanneret, his cousin and partner, also be hired as the site architect. Thapar and Verma proposed to have Le Corbusier come and live in India for three years. Le Corbusier balked at the commitment. At the suggestion of an Indian official at The Hague, they accepted that Le Corbusier would visit India twice a year, for one month each. "Your capital can be constructed here. You can rely on us at 35, Rue de Sèvres to produce the solution to the problem," Le Corbusier put it famously.[30]

Le Corbusier's contract noted that his job was to "advise and actively assist" in:
i. the determination of the general style of architecture
ii. preparation of the principal buildings
iii. architectural treatment and control of the prominent features of the new town, such as important roads, street squares, public gardens and water features
iv. landscaping of public areas
v. development and detailing of the Master Plan
vi. working out of a programme of work for the architectural branch[31]

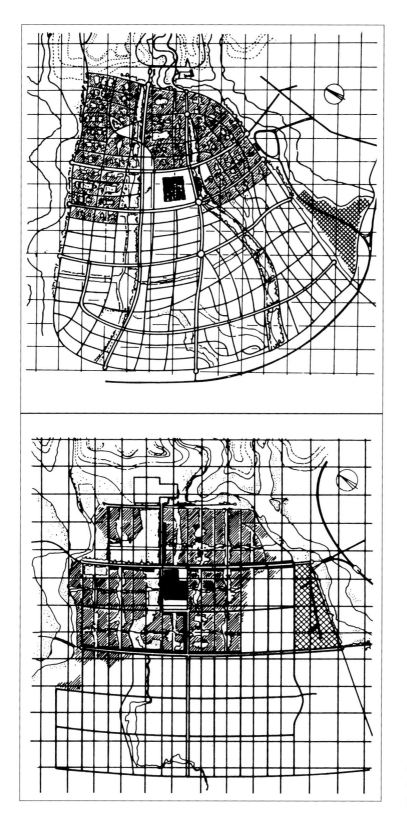

**Fig. 2.3** Drawings comparing Mayer's and Le Corbusier's plans.

When Le Corbusier alighted in Chandigarh, therefore, he was well aware that the scope of his duties was clearly circumscribed, particularly in that the Mayer plan was to be adopted in principle, while he was responsible for advising and assisting only in its development and detailing. Nonetheless, there is evidence that from the outset he took a heavy-handed approach and wanted to influence the city's development as much as possible.[32] He quickly and swiftly took over Albert Mayer's plan and transformed it to reflect his own sense of order and clarity.[33] Maxwell Fry captured the wily Le Corbusier at work, color pencil in hand, surrounded by a Babylon of contentious propositions: "It was a difficult situation. My French was unequal to the occasion. Jeanneret was supernumerary, and Thapar only half aware of what was going forward. Corbusier held the crayon and was in his element."[34]

All the main roads were straightened out, the dimensions and organization of the superblocks were reformatted, a complete hierarchy of circulation was established, the nomenclature was changed, and the Capitol "head" was firmly located in place. What had been named an "Urban Village" in Mayer's plan, Le Corbusier renamed a "Sector." Each sector featured a green strip running north to south, bisected by a commercial road running east to west. The streets were organized in a diminishing hierarchy and labeled V1 through V8: V1: arterial roads that connect one city to another, V2: urban, city roads, V3: vehicular road surrounding a sector, V4: shopping street of a sector, V5: distribution road meandering through a sector, V6: residential road, V7: pedestrian path, V8: cycle track. A light industrial zone was planned at the eastern limit of the city, with an educational zone on the western side (fig. 2.3, plate 4, see page 35).

A drawing comparing the land use of the two plans showed that Mayer's plan utilized 6,908 acres versus Le Corbusier's 5,380 acres (fig. 2.4). Within a matter of days, quite literally, Le Corbusier had increased the city's density by 20 percent by cutting down its area on all fronts; housing, parks, public buildings and roads. Albert Mayer briefly appeared to defend his Master Plan but then chose to quietly disappear. He was no match for Le Corbusier's domineering personality.

Ultimately, Le Corbusier's Master Plan, though not far from the principles of the Garden City movement, was idiosyncratic to his own personality. It suggests that he wanted to make a statement. Stanislaus von Moos has proposed that Chandigarh was intended to imitate Sir Edwin Lutyens's plan for New Delhi:

> From the beginning the Capitol was intended as the Indian answer to the Capitol of New Delhi. Le Corbusier also pa[id] his tribute to the work of Lutyens and Baker: "New Delhi… , the capital of Imperial India, was built more than thirty years ago, with extreme care, great talent and real success. The critics may say what they like; the very act of doing something forces respect—(at least *my* respect)." In fact, as Allen Greenberg noted, Le Corbusier's early studies for the Chandigarh skyline could easily double as illustrations for [a] description of Lutyens' palaces and domes: "The essential ingredients are common—the picturesque skyline of government buildings, the flat intervening city, and the monumental connecting axis." [35] (fig. 2.5)

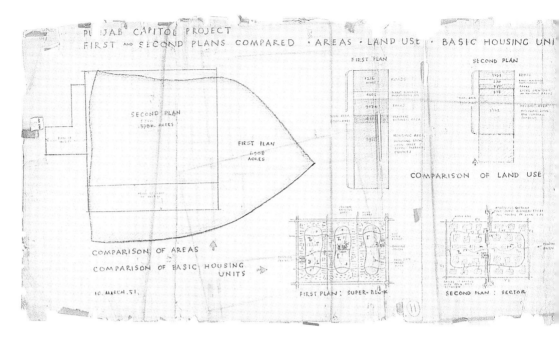

**Fig. 2.4** Drawing comparing areas of Mayer's and Le Corbusier's plans.

Although the visual construction of the two images in von Moos's book are similar, there are important ways in which the urban logics of the two cities are very different. On the same visit to New Delhi where he admired Lutyens's work, Le Corbusier noted that he thought the colonial city's long axial roads were "discouraging" because "Delhi was seen broadly, with unity and discipline. … Chandigarh is the rejection of discipline … the 7V's [the road system of Chandigarh] are interpreted with regret [my translation of the French "douleur"] = not smiling." (3#620)

While Lutyens's layout was dedicated to the scopic interests of axial planning and was meant for the theatrical staging of the horse-drawn but stately vehicles of the imperial government, Le Corbusier's rectilinear road layout was conceived, as he expressed it, "avec douleur." That is "with regret"; it had to be put there. In fact, Le Corbusier noted that in Chandigarh the "pedestrians must be channeled through the little valleys, sinuous walkways and picturesque trees." (2#344) This was his interpretation of a modern Indian way of life:

> [In India] people use their legs: pedestrians. Walking 1/2 hour or more, men and women, straight. Joy of walking, not [being] tired, Chandigarh a walking city and no cars. The pedestrian is alone in the V4s and V7s. … Pierre [Jeanneret] thinks that the Indian people will be caught up in that passion of the automobile, "which is the mark and beauty of the age." No, for some, there is only the need to escape through the automobile because in the West life is crazy. At Chandigarh people will walk without automobile and New York's fifth ave and 42nd street will be grotesque. Calm, dignity, contempt for envy: Perhaps

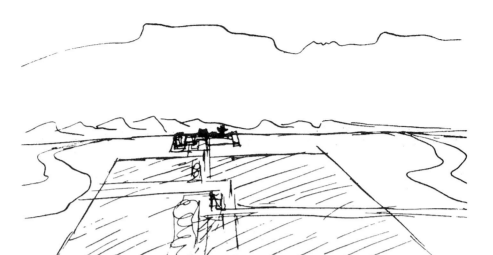

187. Le Corbusier, sketch of Chandigarh with Capitol complex at the city's "head," ca. 1952 (from *Oeuvre complète*)

188. New Delhi; aerial view of the King's Way and Capitol Buildings in the distance (from Butler, *Sir Edwin Lutyens*)

**Fig. 2.5** Page 271 from von Moos 1985, comparing a sketch of Chandigarh by Le Corbusier with an aerial image of Sir Edward Lutyens's New Delhi.

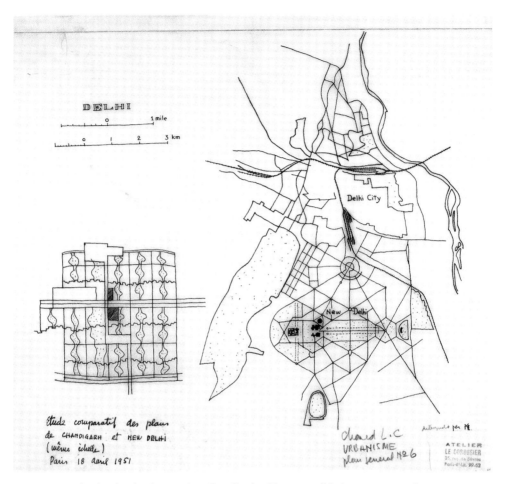

Fig. 2.6 Le Corbusier drawing juxtaposing Chandigarh with New Delhi. (25#46#29051)

India is capable of maintaining herself at this point and establishing herself at the head of civilization. (2#362-3)

If one read this passage out of context, one might think that Chandigarh was a pedestrian heaven, "a walking city and no cars." A quick look at Le Corbusier's Master Plan shows that its basic form is determined by a rectilinear road layout, optimized for the automobile and hardly for the pedestrian. There are long green belts nestled safely within the sectors that are a haven for pedestrians (the V7s), but the fundamental character of the city is drawn from the requirements of motorization.[36] Indeed, as their plans are determined by a rigid road layout, New Delhi and Chandigarh are in fact similar. Le Corbusier himself had the plans of the two cities drawn up in juxtaposition (fig. 2.6).

The passage from Le Corbusier's sketchbook seems ironic and sarcastic. He is fanaticizing, projecting onto the V4s and the V7s an excess of expectations that they in reality could not sustain. The *douleur* in the passage, I would suggest, is signaled by the quotation marks around the description of the automobile as the "mark and beauty of

**Plate 1** The Assembly. (Photograph by Navneet Saxena)

**Plate 2** The High Court. (Photograph by the author)

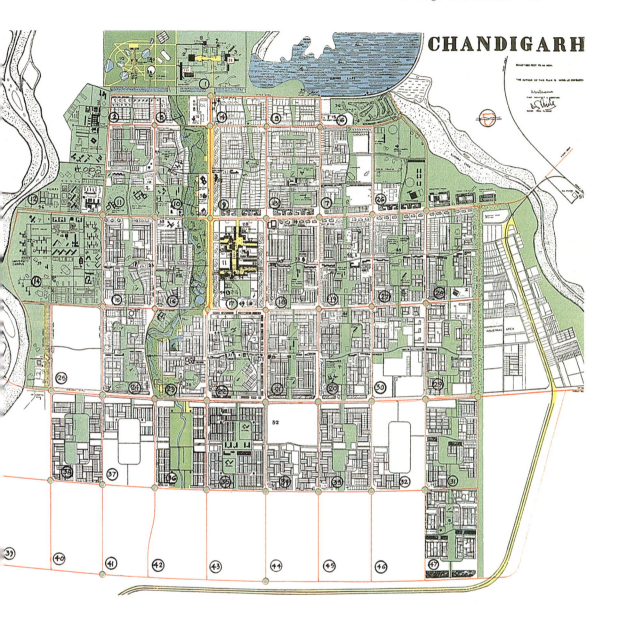

**CHANDIGARH**

**Plate 4** The Chandigarh Plan.

Left:
**Plate 3** Sketch for Type-C housing by Matthew Nowicki.
(Chandigarh Museum Archives)

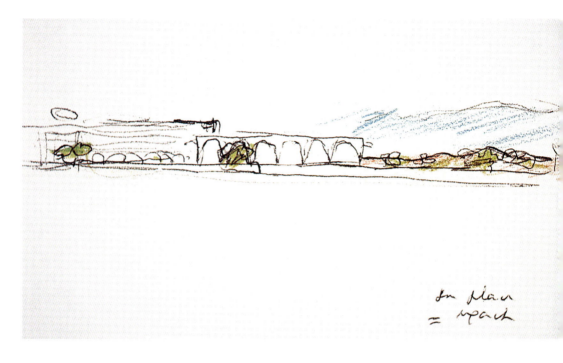

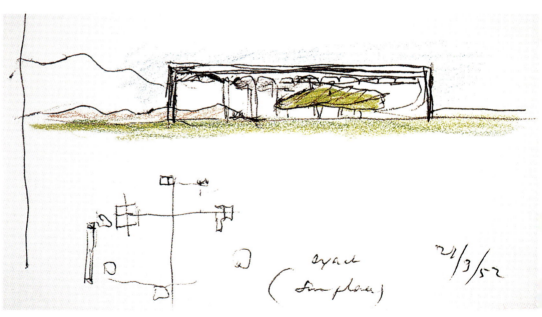

**Plate 5** Le Corbusier sketches showing the final positioning of the Capitol Buildings. (2#722-723)

**Plate 6** Nek Chand's Rock Garden.
(Photograph by the author)

Plate 7 View of the Assembly with the Enamel Door from the central esplanade.
(Photograph by the author)

Plate 8 The Enamel Door, exterior view.
(Photograph by Philip Lehn)

**Plate 9** The Capitol Complex measured against the Himalayas.
(Photograph by the author)

**Plate 10** View of the Secretariat from the edge,
"ploughing through a sea of green."
(Photograph by the author)

**Plate 11** The Assembly roof with its solar sculpture,
derived from the Janter Manter in New Delhi.
(Photograph by Philip Lehn)

Plate 12 The Assembly reflected in the water pools, without an external frame.
(Photograph by Philip Lehn)

Plate 13 View of the Assembly portico with reflection.
(Photograph by Philip Lehn)

**Plate 14** View of the Assembly from the roof of the Secretariat.
(Photograph by Norman Johnston)

**Plate 15** The Open Hand.
(Photograph by the author)

13

Plate 16 Genesis of the Hand.
(From Le Corbusier [c.1950–60], p. 13)

CHANDIGARH 202
OUR CITY IN OUR HAN

Plate 17 An adaption of the Open Hand in a local graphic.
(Photograph by the author)

**Plate 18** Swiss 10-franc bill, front.    **Plate 19** Swiss 10-franc bill, back.

**Plate 20** A Kansal woman walking from the Assembly to her village.
(Photograph by the author)

the age." They indicate a certain distancing, a regretful embrace of the power of the automobile, that "crazy passion" that Le Corbusier himself had been caught up in during his own life.[37]

In pitting New York against India, Le Corbusier is, in fact, not comparing civilizations as much as he is hoping for a contrast in his own experiences in the two places. The intersection of New York's Fifth Avenue and Forty-Second Street is very close to the United Nations building, a project in which Le Corbusier had initially been a central player. He had wanted to make the UN his demonstration skyscraper project in the United States, located on the West Coast in a field of green, lifted off the ground with automobile traffic passing underneath it. Vested real estate interests, however, insisted on having the project built in New York and even refused to allow the token gesture of a street running under the building. In response, Le Corbusier bitterly walked away from the project just before he came to Chandigarh.

Chandigarh was Le Corbusier's opportunity to fulfill his ideas, and he clearly projected onto India—because its "people use their legs"—the chimerical possibility that it would establish itself as the alternative United Nations "at the head of civilization." This was an aspiration for modern India that Nehru certainly shared.

Le Corbusier, however, was unable to execute his full image of a city "at the head of civilization." Other than the Master Plan, the actual housing of the city was not what he wanted it to be. Le Corbusier's vision is contained in the archived transcription of the very first meeting of the new design team in Paris on 6 December 1950. After a preliminary introduction, Le Corbusier peremptorily announced to the rest of the team: "My part of the work will then be to build a 'Block of Buildings,' a 'Dwelling Unity' which already exists, that can be experimented on the spot and will be one of the many 'Dwelling Unities' which you will build over there. I would also like to construct one or two public buildings so as to make use of my personal experience."[38]

"Dwelling Unity" is the English transcriber's literal translation of "Unité d'Habitation." The sustained proposition of years of original research into urban living, Le Corbusier's famous *Unités* were models of integrated vertical living. Lifted clear off the ground plane, like his proposed UN tower, they were designed to emphasize their relationship with the sun and the sky and their freedom from the ground. He doggedly and largely unsuccessfully pursued his Unités everywhere he went. The late 1950s saw the construction of the few that ever were realized. With those just behind him, Le Corbusier no doubt wanted to see more in Chandigarh.

None, however, was constructed. Maxwell Fry records:

> There was an episode that I have never been able successfully to explain, which concerns the distribution of population over the plan sector. We had accepted as something unshakable and inevitable the hierarchic disposition of the population from rich to poor, downward from the Capitol, and we could with no great difficulty have distributed the total of 150,000 over the plan. But Corbusier with some secrecy worked feverishly on a sort of computerization, some system he had in his mind, that would present us with the

mosaic law of the matter, and somewhere in this computation was the hint of a row of high-rise buildings low down in the plan.

They never rose. Whether Thapar scotched them or not I never knew; I knew only that the incomprehensible figures were not to my knowledge applied to the plan, which it was clear from the beginning was to be a poor state's capital in two dimensions, with no two-grade intersections in our lifetime.[39]

Le Corbusier's Unités, or any derivatives from them, were simply not part of the neocolonial housing schema, neatly divided into hierarchical sectors and housing types, that had been predetermined by Fletcher and Verma. Early in the project, Le Corbusier did design some houses for the lowest of the thirteen types of houses developed in Chandigarh for the peons, homes of 1,200 square feet. With each unit consisting of a simple arrangement of a veranda, two bedrooms, a kitchen, an open-air water closet, and an "Indian-style" toilet, each unit had open-air space in front and back as extensions of the house and was surmounted by a secondary parasol roof to keep it cool. The emphasis of the design, Le Corbusier noted, was on "sun, space and greenery" and a mixture of open sky and covered spaces conversing with the brick-paved streets that were to be completely pedestrian. The units were placed side by side and back to back ensuring contiguity and economy of construction while ensuring "absolute privacy." Le Corbusier's referent for the designs, however, was again the Unités. "It is the same principle which was employed in the large apartment blocks (at Marseilles for example)," Le Corbusier noted, "where on 17 floors the apartments are contiguous and of the same lay-out."[40]

None of these homes was constructed either. Only Jeanneret, Fry, and Drew, assisted by the Indian architects, designed the fourteen housing types, catering to the whole range of governmental employee incomes. In his collected works, "the Œuvre," Le Corbusier was at pains to distance himself from the authorship of the city's residential architecture, stating bitterly:

It must be said … that Chandigarh's program of construction was established by high officials, who, having made their studies at Oxford, have known and often appreciated the English civilization. Chandigarh is a horizontal city [and not a vertical one as the Unités would have established]. The Oxfordian program comprises thirteen categories of individual dwellings, from that of the peon to that of a government minister.[41]

Over the years, Le Corbusier and P. L. Verma did in fact become good friends, and Le Corbusier came to champion the importance of Verma in making the Capital project happen. However, when Verma asked Le Corbusier to design his own house in early 1955, Le Corbusier refused and asked Verma to "trust" Jeanneret with the project. Le Corbusier in the meantime did design two houses for industrialists in Ahmedabad, but he clearly did not want to be associated with any residential construction in Chandigarh.[42]

While the "preparation of the principal buildings" was undertaken at 35 Rue de Sèvres in Paris with great care and revision, all his other responsibilities—the "programmer of work for the architectural branch," the "architectural treatment of the prominent features of the new town," and the "landscaping of public areas"—were essentially neglected by Le Corbusier, with a few drawings with guidelines providing the main principles. Later in 1957, when the question of developing a third phase for the city to meet the increased population was being discussed, he once again proposed that the populations of phases I and II be combined in the first, which could be achieved by densification of the city through vertical construction.[43] But that proposal was also unsuccessful.

In the course of his battles with the "Oxfordian program," Le Corbusier also took his case to Nehru, who was quick to take up the cause. In April 1952, after a visit to the Chandigarh site, Nehru wrote a memorandum on "Housing," in which he reported:

> In the course of a conversation with M. Corbusier, he told me that he was surprised and somewhat unhappy at the way we copied foreign models in our buildings and houses, regardless of our own climate and environment. We had got so used to the Anglo-Saxon approach, which was largely based on foreign engineers who had received their training in foreign countries, that we tended to forget that India was somewhat different from these countries of the West. I think that there was a great deal in what M. Corbusier told me. … I am writing this note to draw attention to … what M. Corbusier suggested, i.e. all our building conceptions, small or big, should be thought of more in terms of Indian conditions.[44]

And in the same memo Nehru at the end quietly noted that "our P. W. D. [Public Works Department] rules, more specifically in regard to cheap housing will have to be revised completely."[45]

Later, speaking at a seminar on architecture organized by the Lalit Kala (Fine Arts) Academy in New Delhi, Nehru was far more outspoken in his critique of the ingrained bureaucratic procedures of the Public Works Department. The *Times of India*, the leading national newspaper, reported:

> Mr. Nehru did some plain speaking over the role of the PWD and those of the States which stood like an "impregnable fort" in the way of creative architecture. The PWD had its own outmoded notions of building and architecture, he said. If any thinking creative architect dared to defy its specifications, woe betide him.[46]

Yet, in spite of all their attempts and displeasure, neither Nehru nor Le Corbusier was able to significantly effect the development of the fundamental character of the residential neighborhoods of the city. Other than "rectifying"[47] Mayer's plan and determining the essential architectural zoning of the principal streets of Chandigarh, Le Corbusier was not able to transform the basic development of the Master Plan or its housing provisions. He was effectively challenged and checked by other architects on the

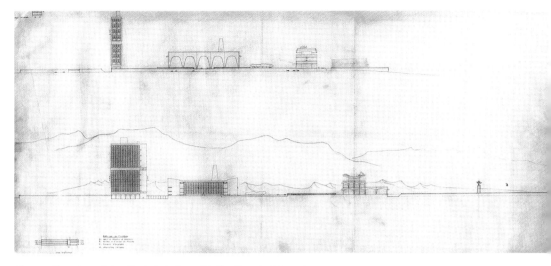

**Fig. 2.7** Elevation of the Capitol skyline with the Secretariat as skyscraper.

team, backed in no small measure by the bureaucracy which oversaw every aspect of the project.[48] It seems that even Jeanneret was not in favor of his cousin's urban plans. Years later Le Corbusier bitterly spoke of the "betrayal" of Fry and Jeanneret. (3#882)

In response to the "scotching" of his multistory ideas for housing, Le Corbusier withdrew from effective participation in the further development of the city. The consequence was the effective dismantling of the relationship between the Capitol and the rest of the city by Le Corbusier.

In the earliest stages, Le Corbusier designed the Capitol to dominate the city—its appropriate head, as proposed by the Master Plan. To achieve this, an important role was to be played by the Secretariat, the largest of the buildings. One of the earliest drawings of 20 June 1951 shows the Secretariat as a skyscraper silhouetted against the mountains with the Assembly flanking it on one side (fig. 2.7). Four months later, after the proposal to build the Secretariat as a skyscraper was turned down by city bureaucrats, a drawing dated 25 December 1951 shows the building as a long, low-rise structure[49] (fig. 2.8). A look at the accompanying plan makes it clear that the Secretariat is positioned almost at the edge of the city. Consequently, if built it would have appeared from the city like a long wall against the mountains. There are no visible obstructions, so the Assembly, the Governor's Palace, the High Court, and the Open Hand would also have been visible at variable depths. Conversely, it is obvious that the city would have also been visible from the Capitol. Thus it would seem that until December 1951, at least, the Capitol enjoyed a visually unimpeded relationship with the city.

The first hint of an altered priority is indicated in the sketchbooks, where we see Le Corbusier's decision to turn the Capitol away from the city. A sketch of November 1951 shows that he was wondering whether it would not be better to turn the Secretariat at right angles[50] (fig. 2.9). This sketch is accompanied by another one which shows a transverse section of a "dune." The accompanying text makes the intention of this dune

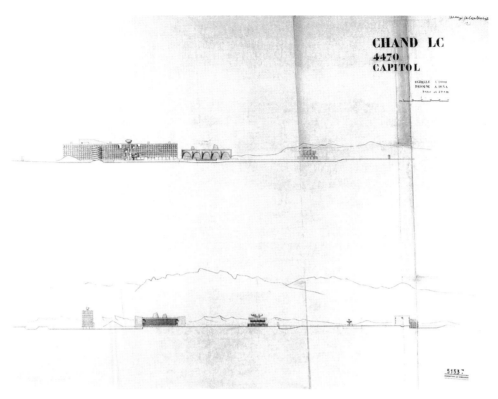

Fig. 2.8. Elevation of the Capitol skyline with the Secretariat laid flat. (22#19#5142)

clear—"A small dune 1.5 m. [high] would suffice to put the Himalayas out of the picture. 1 small dune / end of town—beginning of capitol." (2#638) This small dune was transformed into the higher artificial hills of the final design. On 4 March 1952, Le Corbusier made two more sketches studying the two possible positions of the Secretariat in relation to the Assembly. (2#742, 743) He made another pair of sketches on 21 March, in which the four buildings are in their final position (plate 5, see page 36). The finality of these sketches is indicated by the words "Sur place = exact"—"On place = exact."

These two seminal sketches radically redefined the city's relationship to the Capitol Complex. Instead of the Secretariat silhouetted against the Himalayas, there were now the artificial hills (which is what the dune eventually became) that attempted to block out the "real" mountains. Instead of standing at the city's "head," where, to continue the metaphor used earlier, the Capitol should have been, this double move by Le Corbusier ended up decapitating the "head" from the "body." Le Corbusier carefully designed the hills to ensure they accomplished this purpose. He made sections to determine the sight lines that would, at least at the pedestrian's eye-level, make a connection between Capitol and city impossible. (3#23) On one occasion, when some workmen started making a path on top of the hills, he immediately dashed off orders to his Indian assistant Prabhawalkar to have them removed. In his sketchbook he noted the reason—"The city must never be seen." (4#80)

Fig. 2.9. Le Corbusier sketch considering to rotate the Secretariat ninety degrees. (2#637)

These hills thus did more than simply make an enclosure for the Capitol; they also shut the Capitol off from the city. This is the reverse of the Viceroy's Palace's domineering presence in New Delhi. Thus, at Chandigarh Le Corbusier enacted a parodic reversal of the relationship that Lutyens's Capitol had to New Delhi—Lutyens's Capitol was specially designed to dominate the city; at Chandigarh, a wall of artificial hills was erected between the Capitol and the city.

Why did Le Corbusier make this decision? The functionalists might argue that he had to reorient the Secretariat for climactic reasons. In *Marg*, Le Corbusier notes that this building was supposed to act as an "aerator," i.e., it was to be aired by the prevailing winds that blow from the southeast to the northwest.[51] But that is clearly an insufficient reason, for it does not require the artificial hills. I have proposed that Le Corbusier developed an antagonistic relationship toward the city and its architects, and there is evidence that he may have wanted to turn his back on them. But the other reason, I would argue, is that Le Corbusier wanted to hide behind the walls and build his own compensatory universe, as if the brief space of idealization was sufficient to overcome the city of regrets.

# The Rousseauesque Garden of Eden

If Chandigarh was a symbol of a nation's postponed but much anticipated faith in a future—a prophesy you might say—then perhaps the programmatic head of the city—its Capitol—was symbolic of yet another postponed faith. By strategically locating it in the vast open plain north of the city, bound only in the further north by the overwhelming Himalayan mountains, Le Corbusier created a visually bounded plan, a veritable tabula rasa, upon which, with patience, persistence, and dogged perseverance, this aloof "Master," who carried the air of a prophet, set about drawing his own image of the preferred destiny of a nation's faith in the future.

Most visitors to Chandigarh, however, generally ignore Le Corbusier's Capitol and gravitate instead to what is known as the Rock Garden (plate 6, see page 37). Nestled just south of the Capitol, the Rock Garden is located on land that was technically zoned not to be built upon. It was slowly assembled singlehandedly over thirty years by a former road supervisor, Nek Chand, out of the waste dump generated by the construction of Chandigarh. It is an unusual and fascinating assemblage of thousands of human and animal forms staged in a series of freeform courts, cascading one into the other. Every square inch is covered. One is drawn in to touch and caress, almost with a sense of disbelief, the countless broken pipes, bulbs, lavatories, chinaware, electrical fittings, fluorescent lamps, soda water caps, bangles, feathers, plain ordinary rocks, beer bottles, earthen pots, and the innumerable other objects of everyday life that have been cast into sculptures, doors, walls, floors, roofs, columns, and bridges of surreal beauty. Each court is unique, and they all twist and turn like intestines. As one moves from one court to the next, one completely loses orientation; yet, one wanders on, anticipating one surprise after another, delighting in the bizarre surrealism of the whole construction.

The Rock Garden easily attracts the casual tourist and the curious citizen alike, and has become world famous, in spite of its lack of pedigree. In the visible distance, the Capitol by contrast remains unvisited, save by architects on pilgrimage. Vast and abstract, daunting and puzzling, completely open yet spectacularly opaque to comprehension, the Capitol, compared to the bustling Rock Garden, has the appearance, in Curtis's memorable words, "of a colossal, grave, and dignified ruin."[1] The barbed wire and gun-toting paramilitaries that have guarded the Capitol since the mid-1980s do not, of course, help.

Still, the Capitol fascinates as well. In India, to risk a stereotype, one is habitually taught to revere the ruin, not as a historical curiosity, but as the living presence of the aged—even if just from the distance. One tolerates the ruin with a certain irreverent reverence.

Those of us studying architecture in Chandigarh were educated looking up at Le Corbusier with an (ir)reverent eye. The Capitol was hallowed ground. We would often clamor onto the Capitol Esplanade—sidestepping the security, carrying illegal bottles of beer—and wonder with what eyes it was that the Old Man had surveyed the land. What vision had he seen there, to which we as the second generation were apparent heirs? Is there a buried tablet somewhere to clarifying the symbolic content of the Capitol? I ask with something like the merry irreverence of a gravedigger, exhuming the corpse of Le Corbusier's dead mind. Alas, poor Le Corbusier! Think of it as follows: writing as and on behalf of the progeny of Chandigarh, I am asking the commonplace question of the nature of my parentage. You can also think of it as an inquiry into the possibility of miscegenation in Chandigarh.

On 25 September 1961, Le Corbusier wrote a letter asking Jawaharlal Nehru for a list of drawings of useful "symbolic signs" that could be represented on a large enamel door for the Assembly that he said he was going to paint "with his own hands." Le Corbusier noted that he had already gathered information on some signs "exclusively dating from a hundred or a thousand years ago," but he wanted from Nehru some "signs of our actuality." "A mass of signs is not required," he wrote, "but only some of those concerning the ethics, the social [sic] and the politics of the present times."[2]

Although the letter did attempt to flatter Nehru by noting that he was being asked simply to provide the signs because he "knows and can express them," Le Corbusier did not hesitate to add his own abridgement to "our actuality": "I think the world is becoming, through lack of imagination, quite mad. Everything is opened before us; a programme for peace supplies to feed the factories throughout the world and gorge even the insatiable gluttons who would enjoy starting a war to 'make big money.'"[3]

War and big money were two of Le Corbusier's favorite scapegoats, and we will hear more of them in the chapter on the Open Hand. Meanwhile, if Le Corbusier had hoped that the prime minister would reciprocate with his own program for peace to counter those currently catering to war and big money, he must have been disappointed by the response. Nehru replied that he was, as were his friends whom he had consulted, "much at sea … and did not quite know what to suggest in this connection." He also anonymously appended a letter from a "friend," who noted that he "cannot understand how a few symbolic signs can express these things."

Nehru's friend, nonetheless, went on to venture something of a summary of the nation's aspirations. His observations, as one might expect, were cast in terms of nationalist slogans of the Nehruvian nation-state:

> What is characteristic of India today is the aspiration of the people to re-construct our national life. The villages are changing through the application of science and technology and gradual introduction of cooperation. Industries are also changing their character not only through the creation of heavy industries but also by expansion of various types of small and middle scale industries dealing with consumer goods. Still more important, the whole people are on the march and the expansion in education and panchayats [village governments] is only one expression of this urge.
>
> The Asoka Chakra [wheel] in our flag may perhaps in some respects be regarded as a symbol of India today, standing simultaneously for eternal law and continual process.[4]

Nehru's unnamed friend further observed that he had consulted Dr. Radhakrishnan, the president of the country, who also felt "that it would be difficult to express in a few symbolic signs the aspirations of our people." He apologized that he could not "suggest anything more specific" and instead retorted, "M. Corbusier is a futurist and perhaps he wants some geometrical designs, but obviously he must produce them himself."[5]

Concurring with his friend, Nehru forwarded an old speech of his simply as a tangential reference and encouraged Le Corbusier to find the appropriate symbols himself. As a result of his efforts, therefore, Le Corbusier found himself, and perhaps not unexpectedly, labeled the "futuristic" thinker in the eyes of those who hired him, whose job it was to decide on these "signs of our actuality … concerning the ethics, the social and politics of the present." Anticipating the future was after all part of his core job description.

After extensive preparation, Le Corbusier handpainted the 110 enamel panels of the door in March 1962, and they were in Chandigarh by the middle of the year. Two years later, the door was installed in the Assembly Building, and Le Corbusier specifically came to attend its dedication ceremony on 15 April 1964, barely a year before his death.

The Enamel Door is pivoted in the middle and has two paintings, one on the inside and the other on the outside. Each painting consists of fifty-five enameled panels, each 70 by 140 centimeters, making the whole door 7.7 meters tall and 7 meters wide. This massive door is flanked by a smaller conventional door that is clearly intended as the entry for everyday usage. Thus the main enamel door—like the doors of Catholic churches—functions symbolically, marking a presence, stating a purpose, to be actually opened on special occasions only.

The painting that faces into the Assembly is dark and cryptic. It is probably concerned with processes of aesthetic insight. Mogens Krustrup, in his detailed ledger of its codes, has much to say about it.[6] In this chapter I will concentrate on the outside painting that faces the main esplanade, visible from a distance, self-consciously located to draw attention to itself. Rather than concentrating on aesthetic issues, interpreting the symbolism of the painting, we can ascertain some of the ways in which a larger cultural narrative is woven into the aesthetic text.

## The Enamel Door: The Sons of the Sun

The outside painting of the Enamel Door (henceforth referred to simply as "the Door") has a simple compositional strategy. It is conceived by Le Corbusier as a symbolic text.[7] Divided into two equal parts, it describes a landscape with the red and yellow sky above and the green land below. The margin between the two parts itself is split, forming a double band. The upper band is blue and denotes the horizon line with a mountainous silhouette, presumably of the Himalayas. Below it is a yellow and black band, that signifies the two parts of the day. Above the horizonline on the left and right, geography book diagrams signify the solar and lunar cycles, the solstices, and the equinoxes. In the middle, center stage, looming over the entire composition, are two elliptic arches, tracing the trajectories of the summer and the winter sun. The lower half is an idyllic landscape populated with the Modulor Man, animals, natural formations, and other cryptic symbols distributed evenly over the entire surface (plates 7 and 8, see pages 54, 55).

The upper half is fairly easy to decipher. This part of the Door valorizes the role of the sun, the "master" as Le Corbusier called it, "of our lives." This solar symbolism not only continues on the roof of the Assembly's parabaloid, but also accounts for three of the six large "monuments" that Le Corbusier dispersed around the Capitol plain, namely the "24 Solar Hours," the "Course of the Sun Between Two Solstices," and the "Tower of Shade." These monuments, like the Door, were projected by Le Corbusier as "symbols of a high preoccupation—of the major preoccupations in the mind of a constructor."[8] The three solar monuments collectively refer to Le Corbusier's conception of architecture as an instrument, or as a "machine" as he once infamously put it, for integrating human life and habitat with the forces of nature, especially the sun. The essential architectural resolution is contained in the Tower of Shade, located in the middle of the Capitol Esplanade, that consists of an empty shell of *brise soleil* designed to keep the summer sun out, and to let the winter sun in.

As a response to the sun, the Capitol Complex can be interpreted as an interlaced array of sunbreakers—elaborate *brise soleil* arrangements—or solar machines as it were.[9] As such, the symbolic content of the Capitol itself, if one adopts a quasi-primitivistic predilection, could be interpreted as something of a habitat happily accommodated to the sun. One could argue at this point that Le Corbusier's architecture was always nostalgic for the brilliant Mediterranean sun, and that Chandigarh, well in the tropics, was the logical site for the culmination of these solar desires.

The solar symbolism of the Door, however, nurtures connotations that are broader and more cryptic than those pointing to the sun's property as an originator of light and heat. To begin with, they are related to the solar sculptures on the roof of the legislative chamber, at the pinnacle of the Assembly. Here we find two parabolas

**Fig. 3.1** Legislators entering the Assembly through the Enamel Door on the opening day. (From Le Corbusier 1970, p. 84)

depicting once again the path of the summer and the winter sun, juxtaposed against another upward turning spiral derived from a sundial.[10] In his *Marg* article devoted to the Capitol, Le Corbusier noted that the roof of the Assembly was essentially ritualistic in function and was to be used only once a year, on the day of the opening of the Assembly. The purpose of this ritual, Le Corbusier noted rather mysteriously, was to remind the legislator that he was "a son of the sun"[11] (fig. 3.1).

Who are the sons of the sun? What does it mean to be a son of the sun?

Le Corbusier's sketchbooks contain some clues. Perhaps it was only because he did not elicit a full response from Nehru, but at this time Le Corbusier was rereading a book entitled *Les grands initiés* (*The Great Initiates*) by a French late nineteenth-century critic and dramatist, Edouard Schuré.[12] Le Corbusier made a note in his sketchbook to consult *The Great Initiates*, with the intention of retracing what reads like a nebulous connection between Hindu gods, symbolic animals, and events from the Bible:

> On return look again in Schuré *Les Grands initiés*
> Brahma
> bull and lamb
> [And] in Bible
> the prophecy of Ezekiel and Apocalypse. … (4#270)

A clearer connection between Hindu gods and the Bible can be found in *The Great Initiates.* Working his way through an abbreviated and highly personalized recounting of Hindu, Egyptian, Greek, and Judeo-Christian (no Islamic!) myths, Schuré's project in this book is to synthesize the founding myths of these religions into the singularity of his own thesis:

> Beyond the conflicts of history, the wars of cultures, the contradictions of sacred texts, we shall enter the very consciousness of the founders and prophets who gave religions their initial impetus. From above, these men received keen intuition and inspiration, that burning light which leads to fruitful action. Indeed, synthesis pre-existed in them. The divine ray dimmed and darkened with their successors, but it reappears, it shines whenever a prophet, hero or seer returns to his life origin. For only from this point of departure does one see the goal; from the shining sun, the path of the planets.[13]

Schuré's interpretation aspires to a synthetic unity which he believes underlies the essential spirituality of all religions. By Schuré's claim this synthesis "pre-existed," was a priori to his great men, and his task is simply to "uncover" this unity by unfolding a story of the progressive search for the truth that is exemplified in the lives and works of the "great initiates." Perhaps all too predictably, he finds in the figure of Jesus the teleological culmination of a series of "great initiates"—Rama, Krishna, Hermes, Moses, Orpheus, Pythagoras, Plato, Jesus.

It is Schuré's section entitled "India and the Brahmanic Initiation" that identifies the disciples of Krishna as "the Sons of the Sun."[14] These disciples, the Pandavas, are the mythological forefathers of the Aryan tribes that putatively conquered and settled in the plains of North India, where Chandigarh is located. The ancient epic *Mahabharata* recounts that at least one of the Pandavas was indeed born of the hidden union between their mother Kunti and the sun god Surya. According to Schuré, these upper-caste, white-skinned Aryans, the Pandavas, engaged in epic battle with the lower-caste, darker descendants of the moon, the Kauravas. Under Krishna's guidance, the Pandavas were victorious; but final victory was only gained when Krishna, the great initiate, picked his moment of death to proclaim that "the sons of the sun are victorious." With Krishna's death, like that of Jesus, according to Schuré, "a great part of India embraced the cult of Vishnu, which reconciled the solar and the lunar cults in the religion of Brahma."[15]

While some of Schuré's stories are completely fanciful, most are simply re-contextualized interpretations that are intended to mirror Christian teachings or to suggest that they were precursive to Christian theology. One cannot, however, rule out Schuré's argument simply as overzealous Christian claptrap. Schuré is after all writing in the nineteenth century, and his narrative belongs to that ultimately colonizing mind-set that seeks to resolve the plethora of the world's differences through a model of synthesis. For the colonists, one of the justifications of colonization was that it unified a world full of differences and strife in the singularity of the Empire. This synthesizing idea runs deep in western epistemology. Inherently privileging that which unifies over that which differentiates is a Neoplatonic ideal that is echoed and reinforced by monotheistic religions. It is grounded in the belief that ultimately everything must stem from a single truth, and that this essential singularity is the superior philosophical truth. Even as they rejected theology, this principle was also unquestionably adopted by Western Enlightenment thinkers, as for instance in the still commonplace belief that reason and logic are superior to the more cultural claims of society, since the former are claimed to be valid for all humans.

For a Schuré, and later for a Le Corbusier, what is at stake in the claim to a synthesis, therefore, is access to a supposedly higher knowledge that, in being common to all cultures, can be used to represent, without really engaging, an Other. Such claims are self-serving, and although they claim to represent, to speak for the Other, they in fact represent and silence the Other. Whenever applied to other cultures, as they often were, and indeed still are, these principles serve the interests of ideological colonization as they dissolve or at least subordinate difference through the "unity" and singularity of the usually western (i.e., Neoplatonic, monotheistic) ideals they imply.[16]

*The Great Initiates* was given to the young Le Corbusier in 1907 by his mentor, L'Eplattenier, apparently as a farewell gift before the former left for his famous "journey to the East."[17] The book and its prophetic claims were seminal in Le Corbusier's life, and, as his sketchbook evidences, it was one of the texts to which he returned even late in life. Le Corbusier's reference to the "sons of the sun" no doubt was directed to elicit a mythological connection between the Pandavas and the new legislators, invoking them to live up to ancestral ideals. It was an attempt to answer himself the question of the signs of India's "actuality" that he had directed to Nehru.

There is sensible evidence that Le Corbusier also fancied himself an inheritor of the visions and purposes of Schuré's "great initiates." This was certainly the case toward the end of his life. When he came to the Chandigarh site in 1951, Le Corbusier had just finished a chapel at Ronchamp, France; was designing a monastery in La Tourette, France; and was in the midst of writing his autobiographical philosophical manifesto, the *Poem of the Right Angle*. His work carried a prophetic tenor, as if the wandering messiah, conscious of his approaching end, was trying to enact and erect (and even legislate if possible) the signs and symbols of his "faith." He considered himself gifted with an exceptional "sense of the unknown," able to discern and choose between good and evil:

> Since June 1955, they've been requesting from me Catholic + Protestant Churches. …
> I did one [Ronchamp] taking 1 risk[,] the big risk. It's done. I possess a sense of the
> unknown, of the immense space left to man before his imagination, his possible choice

between good and evil. Define the one and the other? A single light, discern and choose. (3#722)

Although he often claimed that he was merely a builder—"I have very human tasks to resolve … there is my hard task" (3#722)—Le Corbusier's sketchbooks and letters are filled with prophetic proclamations such as this taken from *The Final Testament*, the last thing he wrote before he died: "We must rediscover man. We must rediscover the straight line wedding the axis of fundamental laws: biology, nature, cosmos. Inflexible straight line like the horizon of the sea."[18]

The "straight line wedding the axis of fundamental laws" is an aesthetic corollary to the synthetic unity aspired to by Schuré's narrative. It aims to thread a world of difference into the singularity of the supposed immutability of its laws. It is teleological and directed toward a definite end. It preexists, is a priori to, "man"—all men—and its "re-discovery" will enable the "re-discovery" of "man."

Who is the "man" this line will specifically help to "rediscover?" What would be the source of the original "discovery," if there were one? Described within the overlaid folds of this project of discovery linking biology, nature, and cosmos are no doubt the "signs of our actuality," the signs of the Capitol as envisaged by Le Corbusier. In the following I will propose two interrelated answers to these questions. The first stems from the Bible and the other from Rousseau—both of which are close to Le Corbusier's imagination. And the story of their interrelationship, which interests me the most and with which I will end, may be much too familiar for the western reader. Building on the clue from Schuré, the remainder of this chapter, piecemeal, one jigsaw piece at a time, assembles a case history of the hegemony of a synthetic process at work in Le Corbusier's interpretation and representation of Indian culture in the design of the Capitol and the painting of the Enamel Door.

### Stories from the Bible

Le Corbusier is reported to have said that one of the three most important books in his life was the Bible.[19] Since he was a descendant of Albigensian origins, alternative biblical teaching was commonplace in Le Corbusier's childhood. His mother was devout, though his father (who is rarely mentioned by Le Corbusier in his writings) was not. The Albigensians are a relatively obscure religious group, who believe in the inherent duality of the world and who, given their medieval persecution by the Catholic Church, essay to live the romance of perseverance in the face of oppression, an idea that Le Corbusier internalized deeply.

Religious influence is not just a matter of belief or lack thereof. That is, it is not just a matter of the politics of belief—yes or no, in or out. In our secular post-Enlightenment world, religions persist as a pervasive and grounding epistemology. They form an intricately woven mesh of values, beliefs, suppositions and predispositions that underlie, subtend, and envelop one's everyday acts. As such they script our choices and conscript our volition to be trained to behave in a certain way. These operations occur in the minutiae of life, almost subconsciously.

I have quoted some biblical references already, and indeed, once one starts looking for them, one finds that Le Corbusier's writings are replete with them. His conception of "truth"—that critical quest so essential for the "re-discovery of man"—for instance, is also cast in a biblical metaphor emphasizing duality: "In the final account, the dialogue is reduced to man alone, face to face with himself, the struggle of Jacob with the Angel, within man himself! There is only one judge. Your conscience—in other words, yourself."[20]

The wrestling of Jacob and the Angel is a story from Genesis that describes the struggle between Jacob/man and God. When Jacob emerges victorious, he is blessed by the angel with the name Israel, and "he struggles with God." In his modern-day personalized transliteration, Le Corbusier saw this as the battle for the "re-discovery of Man"—and his own life as the courageous march of a modern-day prophet marked by "regularity, modesty, continuity, [and] perseverance":

> I am 77 years old, and my moral philosophy can be reduced to this; in life it is necessary above all to act; and by that I mean to act in a spirit of modesty with exactitude, with precision. The only possible atmosphere in which to carry on creative work is one in which these qualities prevail: regularity, modesty, continuity, perseverance.[21]

As with all such marches, his march was carried out in a land dominated by Evil; when he was working on Chandigarh, Le Corbusier saw his work as something of a crusade against the work of the Devil, who is always devoted to the temptation of material things, to money:

> We must cease preparing for war, the cold war should cease providing a livelihood for men. We must invent, decree the projects of peace. Money is nothing but a means. There is God and there is the Devil—the forces confronting us. The Devil is simply in the way; the world of 1965 is capable of living in peace. There is still time to choose, to equip ourselves rather than to arm.[22]

Toward the end of his life Le Corbusier seems to have developed an exceptional interest in the Apocalypse, and the work of the Devil was prominent in his mind. Without explaining why, Le Corbusier accorded a place of importance to the following in his *Final Testament*: "When I was alone once more, I recalled that admirable line from the Apocalypse: And in the heavens all was still for a while …"[23]

In the Revelation, the heavens were silent for a while when the Lamb opened the seventh and final seal that unleashed gigantic scourges upon the immoral earth—fire, earthquakes, demons, in short the work of the Devil—ending with the final fall of Babylon, that whore of a great city that ruled over the kings of the earth.

The world of the 1950s and 60s, fraught with the atomic anxieties of the Cold War, must certainly have seemed like the advent of the Apocalypse. But the Apocalypse in Christian teleology is always only the proverbial first act of the drama that promises deliverance in its last. The making of Chandigarh was in Le Corbusier's eyes something of an instrument of delivery. As one of the "great initiates," there is a distinct sense that in Chandigarh Le Corbusier aspired to align, or realign as it were, his destiny with that of the "sons of the sun" and to deliver them to salvation; the "wedding of the fundamental laws" was part of this enterprise.

It was an unexpected intervention of destiny that had brought him to Chandigarh, and Le Corbusier imbued that fact with prophetic tenor, as if Chandigarh was something of a god-sent gift, intended to fulfill his historical role. Waiting for the arrival of the Indian officials dealing with the project, he wrote, "It is the hour that I have been waiting for: India, that humane and profound civilization. …"[24]

The "profundity" of Indian civilization for Le Corbusier lay not in its cities or historical architecture, but in the naturalistic primitivism of India's rural culture. Soon after his first visit to Chandigarh, he wrote of the "essential joys of the Hindu principle":

> At the end of the race, 1951 at Chandigarh contact [is] possible with the essential joys of
> the Hindu principle: brotherhood, relationship between the cosmos and living things:
> Stars, nature, sacred animals, birds, monkeys, and cows, and in the village children, adults
> and old people, the pond and the mango trees, everything is present and … poor but
> *proportioned*. (2#448–449)

Le Corbusier repeatedly invoked this rural-cosmic image of India, and it played a foundational role in the final design. "Poor but proportioned": this "brotherhood" of humans, animals, and the earth that is laid out by Le Corbusier describes the conditions of a rediscovered Eden where there is no room for conflict. He couched it in familiar orientalist tropes of eternity and stasis—it was the way of all times in the land of the "sons of the sun":

> It is the way of all times …
> —the eternal animals: the cow, the somber gray buffalo, the (little) ass, the sheep the
>   goat the hog.
> —carting, carrying on the head: dignity, time, waiting.
> —Before the big money! (2#330)

"Avant le big money!" Le Corbusier's eulogies to the labors of these "eternal animals" were not without their political purposes. Le Corbusier repeatedly and insistently inveighed against the "society of money" and its pernicious influences. It was the closefisted policy of this society according to him, that had disabled the "First Machine Age," Le Corbusier's term for the industrial revolution, from fulfilling its promise to fill the hands of all with goods, without selfishness. In the above quote, Le Corbusier used the words "Big Money" in English signifying that the object of his invective was directed against the United States and its capitalist economy—against the "complete bankruptcy of America," and its "society of money." India by contrast appeared for Le Corbusier "with a symbolism of the heart":

> In the complete bankruptcy of America (moral and living) we see the failed conclusion of
> the first machine era … Asia, India appears with a symbolism of the heart—Christ plus
> their own cosmic—(nature)—implanted upon a code of signs = freedom within a human-
> cosmic order. (2#855)

If Evil was associated with power and money (thus Le Corbusier's invective
against the United States), the Good—"poor but proportioned"—in good Christian
tradition was made possible in Le Corbusier's eyes by the material poverty of the poor,
the final inheritors of the earth:

> Joliet-Curie coming back from India told me …
> "Rich people in palaces, and the sidewalks crowded with a mass of atrociously poor
> ones." Not one word of the human splendors to be found everywhere and without class,
> outside of class, relationships without violence. For us[,] for me, all possibilities appear as
> a possible flowering of and as a finally radiant overture to the machine age. The crab, like
> the serpent, discards its skin at the proper season. So it will be with the society of money:
> India, a nation of people who have nothing and a few who have everything. This makes
> for jealousy never surfacing and for material wealth remaining outside [the domain] of
> those spiritual riches [that are] available to all and existing for all. (2#365)

Since wealth creates jealousy, the conditions of poverty, for Le Corbusier,
preserve "those spiritual riches [that are] available to all and existing for all." This is the
eternal "richness" of the land of the "sons of the sun." And in the end, in this eschatology,
the poor, like the crabs shedding their skin at the proper season, shall inherit the earth.
Then India will flower as the final overture to the machine age. These are the possibilities
that Le Corbusier sets himself to actualize in Chandigarh.

Thus one finds that it is the "eternal" rural landscape, not the emerging
metropolis of Chandigarh, that is the declared referential context of Le Corbusier's
Capitol. In the opening paragraph of his *Marg* article, Le Corbusier, in carefully recorded
detail, wrote that the Capitol was placed at the top of the town *not* to take advantage of
its proximity, but the very reverse: to turn its back on it, to nestle instead in a "magistral
bucolic symphony"; "villages, sugar-cane fields, wheat fields, colza fields, etc., ploughings
and pastures, peasants at work":

> The Capitol was placed at the top of the town so as to take good advantage of the
> presence of the mountains, the hills and the agricultural life (villages, sugar-cane fields,
> wheat fields, colza fields, etc., ploughings and pastures peasants at work, cartings, cows,
> oxen and bulls), this millennial activity touching the Capitol, separated by one single pit of
> 4 meters width preventing confusion, but connecting modern times to the magistral
> bucolic symphony. It had been necessary to discover, see and realize this prodigious
> contact, prepare the regulations which will perpetuate this "unequalled" state of matters: a
> treasure of teaching and poetry.[25]

"Avant le big money," the Capitol therefore is the designed ("discover, see and realize") prodigious contact between modern times and a "magistral bucolic symphony," "a treasure of teaching and poetry."

How exactly is this manifested in the Capitol? While the Capitol buildings are clearly representations of the modern times, where is the "bucolic symphony?" The "one single pit of four meters" meant to be "preventing confusion" is easy to identify. Unbuilt, in the plans it is located along the northern edge of the Capitol and functions like the ha-ha wall in English romantic landscape gardens; i.e., it would prevent animals from crossing but would not be visible at the human eye level. It is a clever device, intended to preserve a fixed hierarchy in a landscape construed as a painting. But what is the "unequalled" landscape it perpetuates?

### The Capitol Village

All the land around the Capitol was reserved. No one could build there, and Le Corbusier very carefully regulated all the development in that area.[26] With the city screened off to the south, the entire landscape is a world unto itself. To the east there is an artificial lake, created by a long dam on an intermittent rivulet. Although the Capitol

Fig. 3.2 Le Corbusier sketch noting that the Capitol is to be closed off from the city. (2#951)

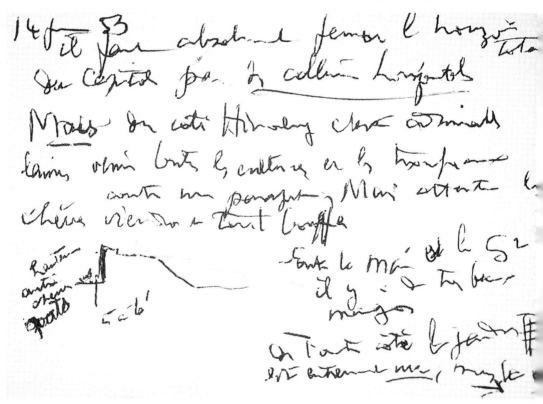

buildings form an attractive silhouette from the lake, the High Court and the artificial hills screen the view from the Capitol toward the west. On the eastern side, the long expanse of the Secretariat merges into the Assembly and definitively screens the view. Centered on the main esplanade, the Capitol buildings on the east and west act as theatre screens, focusing the spectator's view toward the open northern expanse. They are stage sets—props—pointing to the north. These are the views Le Corbusier sketched and annotated "sur place = exact"–"on place = exact." The long silhouette of the Himalayan mountains in the distance is presumed to be their primary focus.

To the north the land extends for a long while before it reaches the foothills. Visitors often comment that the Capitol is fundamentally incomplete because the Governor's Palace (later the Museum of Knowledge) was supposed to occupy the center of this vista. Without it, they argue, the landscape is blank, uninhabited.[27] Without the dramatic Governor's Palace, the Open Hand, one of the monuments that Le Corbusier designed for the Capitol, seems to be the only actor-hero in the vast northern expanse, bound by the Himalayas, framed by the other Capitol buildings.

The view to the north, however, is *not* "empty"—it is, in fact, inhabited and very visibly so. Not only are there agricultural fields that are ploughed by a multitude of the

**Fig. 3.3** Sketch on the facing page of Le Corbusier's sketchbook, stating that the "view of the existing village is intact and beautiful." (2#952)

"eternal animals"—but more importantly, there is a full-fledged thriving village there! Seventeen villages were cleared to make place for Chandigarh, and Le Corbusier had full control over what remained and what did not in the Capitol. On one occasion, when the Indian army proposed building their headquarters on the distant hills, Le Corbusier moved Jawaharlal Nehru to try and have it stopped. The preservation of this particular village, therefore, would not have been outside his intention. Indeed, as a quiet note in his sketchbook betrays, the village was in fact carefully designed into the composition of the Capitol:

> June 14, 1953
>
> it is absolutely necessary to close off the total horizon of the Capitol by means *of* horizontal hills
>
> But on the side of the Himalayas its admirable [...] let the cultures and flocks run right up
>
> Between the Hand [and] the G[overnor's Palace] there are very handsome mango trees
>
> [And] on the other side the garden is completely naked, but the view\\
>
> but the view of the existing village is intact and beautiful. (figs. 3.2, 3.3) (2#951–952)

**Fig. 3.4** View of workers published by Le Corbusier in his *Complete Works*. (From Le Corbusier 1957, p. 61)

Fragment de la façade principale avec les petites Cours de Justice   Main façade with the little courts   Hauptfassade mit den kleinen Gerichtssälen

"Intact and beautiful," this village, nowadays called Kansal, is located just to the northeast of the site of the Governor's Palace, north of the Assembly. For a champion of modern times, Le Corbusier's interest in this village was exceptional. He visited it often, made sketches of its walls and animals and even had a photograph of the Assembly taken from the village pond published in the *Œuvre complète*.[28] Le Corbusier carefully recorded the view of the village and went to extraordinary lengths to ensure that the village would be preserved. He made sure no hills and craters would be made that would block out the village. (4#466)

It was as if the *village* and not the city, and not even the central esplanade was the privileged locus of the Capitol. The village, it is important to note, is not mentioned prominently in Le Cobusier's publications on Chandigarh. When one looks through the *Œuvre complète*, however, one does notice that its pages on Chandigarh are thickly populated with photographs of the migrant and local rural workers who built the Capitol: there are turbaned Sikhs bending steel, children sitting around on the ground, a donkey driver brandishing his cane, and innumerable veiled women carrying loads on their heads. These photographs are uncaptioned, mute, but all-pervasive, occupying

**Fig. 3.5** Views of workers published by Le Corbusier in his *Complete Works*. (From Le Corbusier 1957, p. 87)

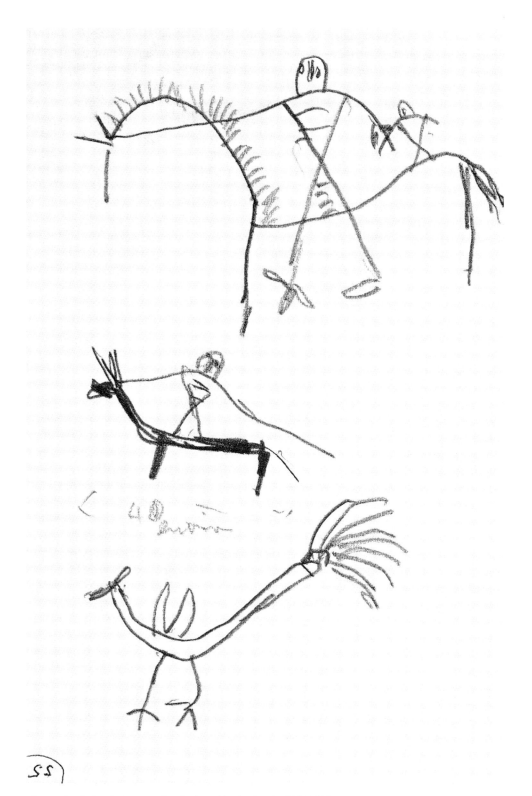

**Fig. 3.6** Le Corbusier's copy of a donkey driver's sketch. (3#1093)

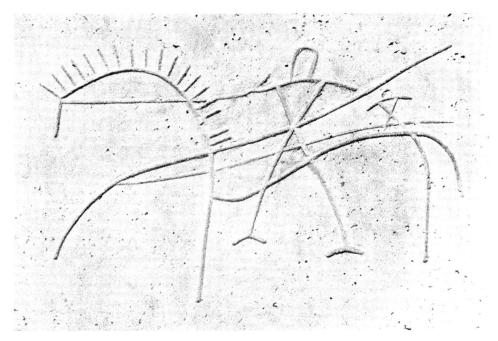

**Fig. 3.7** A concrete cast on the Lake's promenade of the donkey driver's sketch. (From Le Corbusier 1965, p. 113)

numerous pages in the *Œuvre complète*. By contrast there are few photographs of the urban residents, the legislators, and judges who were actually to occupy the Capitol (figs. 3.4, 3.5).

It was as if the rural workers were the idealized occupants of the Capitol. Le Corbusier no doubt was transferring onto these rural workers his own fantasy of a "poor but proportioned" state of being. Le Corbusier spoke no Hindi, and they no English, far less any French. Actual contact must have been infrequent but, I suspect, of great import for Le Corbusier. The only direct evidence of contact one finds in Le Corbusier's sketchbooks is the occasional Hindi text or drawing pencilled in by an unknown hand (figs. 3.6, 3.7). Le Corbusier did make much of one particular drawing that he saw a donkey driver etch into the fresh concrete. He had it copied and cast on a large commemorative block poured in place along the promenade on the lake. I will come back to it in a moment.

### The Garden of Eden

We can now return to the painting on the Enamel Door to complete our interpretation. If in Le Corbusier's world the peasants were the imaginary "real" occupants of the Capitol, what is the larger cultural text that authors and authorizes this transference? In the painting on the Door, time, space, and abstract principles are woven together in a transformed purist vocabulary, narrativizing in visual terms, I would propose, the story of origin from the Bible. Genesis describes the garden of Eden as being made by God by cordoning off the desert and cultivating the land and growing fruit trees. Through the garden flows the river that irrigates it. Man is made from the earth, followed by the animals, and finally Eve, who is created from Adam's rib. In the very center of the garden stands the forbidden tree of knowledge.[29]

The lower half of the Enamel Door, backgrounded with green, describes this Edenic landscape. Starting at the upper left side, we find the vision of an uncultivated desert landscape, dominated by a red, flying, falcon-like bird, a symbol of the original spirit. At the desert's edge at the threshold of the green landscape stands Le Corbusier's abstracted human figure, the upright Modulor Man. The red of the falcon-spirit, as that of the upright Man, signifies their contiguity with the (red) heaven above. This, then, is a picture of the barren earth, and of the Holy Spirit and Adam made from earth in the image of God. The river is present in its terrestrial meanders on the left and as an abstracted ecosystem on the right. The animals are there, performing double symbolic duty—the turtle (also a symbol of dwelling), the bull (Le Corbusier's favorite signature), the fish, and, of course, the serpent.[30] In the center is the proverbial tree of knowledge, flowering into the fruits of knowledge, here heraldic signs. The tree marks the pivotal axis on which the Door turns, defining a strong vertical axis in the center in the form of an upward rising event reinforced by the isosceles triangle in the background.[31]

To claim that there is an Edenic subtext inscribed onto the surface of the Enamel Door and by extension onto the Capitol plain, is not, of course, to claim that Le Corbusier developed fundamentalist Christian tendencies toward the end of his life. Seeking to "re-discover the fundamental laws," Le Corbusier's utopian modernity derives its imagery from a resurrected Eden. It is ultimately a secularized, redemptive eschatology.[32]

There was always a redemptive thrust in Le Corbusier's architecture, which intended to reestablish, to regain the proper place, the proper home of man. This is what one means when one refers to him as a universal, utopian thinker. It is important to remember, even at the risk of simplification, that a utopian, redemptive eschatology is not a fundamental "Hindu principle." It is a modern western epistemological stance, derived from the West's Judeo-Christian-Islamic heritage and its vision of paradise. This is something that is of obvious importance for, but perhaps not only obvious to, a postcolonial scholar familiar with the other side of the epistemological divide. Like Le Corbusier, most canonical modern architects were also utopian, and their rhetoric, if not always their projects, was explicitly redemptive, marching toward visions of social transformation of one kind or another. That Le Corbusier's Chandigarh should fall within this agenda is therefore not unexpected.

What remains of interest is understanding the manner in which the rural workers of the Capitol village—the idealized object of redemption ("the Hindu principle")—are represented in the process, i.e., how they help to *verify* modernism's utopian claims.[33]

The clue, of course, lies in their latent potential for redemption, for deliverance into modern civilization.

## Journey to Question the Naked Man

In his *Marg* article, Le Corbusier spoke of the "pit"—the ha-ha trench—that was meant to prevent "confusion" between "modern times" and the "bucolic symphony." A

clue about what the "confusion" might be, and how it could be transcended can be found in Le Corbusier's untranslated 1928 text *Une Maison—Un Palais*. This book is his explanatory text for the 1927 competition for the League of Nations building on Geneva's Lac Léman.[34] The cover of the book makes the structure of Le Corbusier's claim clear: the drawing of a primitive house (*une maison*) is drawn in equivalent comparative juxtaposition to an axonometric drawing of the League of Nations (*un palais*). The graphic layout repeats the syntax of the title: une maison—un palais. The hyphen, like the ditch in the Capitol, separates and connects the maison and the palais (fig. 3.8).

**Fig. 3.8** The "hyphenated" cover of *Une Maison—Un Palais.*

Le Corbusier's argument in this book is not, as a contemporary quick reading of the graphic organization of the cover might suggest, to highlight the contrast between the two. On the contrary, the point is to underscore their connection: the palais is the same as the maison, it is merely a matter of scale, of seeing things rightly. The hyphen is meant to underscore a continuity and not to state a contradiction. The fundamental connection between them is that they are both freely and fully nestled in "the magistral bucolic symphony." Whereas the maison is "naturally" at home in its bucolic landscape, the contemporary palais must be made to fit into its landscape. Le Corbusier proposes to do this by lifting the palais on columns, or "*pilotis*" as he called them, and liberating the ground plane. Thus, the significance of the *pilotis* is not that it lifts the palais off the ground, but that the ground is *liberated* from having to

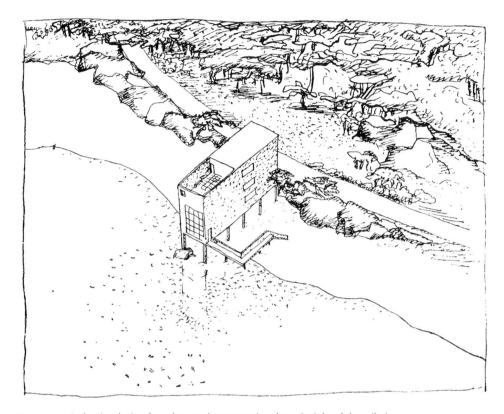

Fig. 3.9 Le Corbusier design for a house demonstrating the principle of the *pilotis*.

bear the immense burden of the building. It is the project's political claim that modern technology—reinforced concrete—is what enables this redemption of the ground plane (fig. 3.9).

In a discussion of his "5 points of architecture" in the *Œuvre complète*, Le Corbusier calls the liberation of the ground by pilotis the act that enables the "restitution" of the ground plane.[35] Restitution is a moral-legal term that specifies the return of something lost to its rightful owner. It implies the reestablishment of the right order, as it once existed. This rightful owner, in the case of Le Corbusier's architecture, is none other and none less than Rousseau's noble savage, "l'homme naturel." Although Le Corbusier generally spoke in terms of the absolute generality of "man," the identity of this "man"— displayed by the raised hand and upright figure of the Modulor Man—as that of Rousseau's noble savage has been established by Adolf Max Vogt in his *Le Corbusier, the Noble Savage*.

Vogt notes that Le Corbusier mentions Rousseau in *Precisions*, a text he wrote on a lecture tour in Brazil.[36] This reference occurs in the midst of a description of the pastoral landscape of the Geneva project that Le Corbusier does not "want to disturb." It is not that different from the "bucolic symphony" of Chandigarh's Capitol:

> Finally, here is the project of the World Center of Geneva … the pilotis furnish such a
> powerful poetry that I feel incapable of making it felt in a few words to a new public. The

site is a sort of acropolis, dominating the horizon in four marvelous directions, three of different mountain ranges, the fourth of the perspective of the upper lake. The plateau is in reality made up of softly rolling country, surrounded by immense sloping lawns, dotted with gigantic trees, the object of Genevan pride. *Herds of cattle graze here and there. I do not want to disturb this moving rural sight that recalls the sentimental pages of Jean-Jacques Rousseau.*

Nevertheless, I choose the site of gigantic buildings. … I conserve the grass and the herds, the old trees, as well as the ravishing views of landscapes, and above them, at a certain level, on a horizontal slab of concrete, on top of the pilotis descending to their foundations, I raise the limpid and pure prisms of utilitarian buildings; I am moved by a high intention, I proportion the prism and spaces around them; I compose in the atmosphere. Everything counts; the herds, the grass, the flowers in the foreground on which one walks caressing them with one's eyes, the lake, the Alps, the sky … *the divine proportions.*

And thanks to the pilotis, on this acropolis destined for meditation and for intellectual work, the natural ground remains, the poetry is intact.[37]

Thanks to the pilotis, thus, the "poetry" of "divine proportions" that recalls the "sentimental pages of Jean-Jacques Rousseau" remains "intact." Rousseau's basic argument, as is well known, was that man was good by nature and became evil only through the corruption of institutions and the profit motives created by the concept of private property. The sentimental pages that Le Corbusier refers to occur repeatedly in Rousseau's essays and novels and are designed, through a counterfactual imagining of the earliest primeval landscapes, to evoke the original nature of man, before being "civilized," before, that is, the fall. In *On the Origin of Inequality Among Men*, Rousseau depicts this counterfactual world as working in harmony with nature:

Differences of the soil, of the climate, and the seasons determined difference in the way of life. Barren years, long and hard winters, short summers that burn everything, demanded of men new abilities. Along with the seas and rivers they invented fishing rods and fishing hooks and became fisher men and fish-eaters. In the forests they made bows and arrows and became hunters and warriors. In the cold countries they covered themselves with furs of the animals they had killed. The thunderstorm, a volcano, or some lucky chance acquainted them with fire, a new resource against the hardship of winter; they learned to conserve the element, then to light it themselves, and finally to cook with it the meat that they previously had eaten raw.[38]

As long as they lived in their "hut out in the country," using technologies that were integrated with nature and there was no concept of private property, the natural conditions remained. But the moment private property was introduced, "slavery and misery sprang up on top of the fields and grew along with the harvests":

As long as men were satisfied with their hut out in the country, as long as they limited themselves to sewing their clothes out of animal skins with thorns and bone fragments, to adorning themselves with feathers and sea shell, to painting their bodies with different pigments, to improving and decorating their bows and arrows, to building with sharp stones some fishing boats, or to making some simple musical instruments; in short, as long as they produced objects that did not need the collaboration of many hands, *they lived as free, healthy, decent, and happy as they could be by nature*, and enjoyed together the pleasures of independent interchanges. But from the moment when man needed the help of others, when he realized that it was useful for one single person to have on hand supplies for two, then equality disappeared. Private property was introduced, labor became necessary, and the vast forest turned into open fields that had to be watered by human sweat. Slavery and misery sprang up on top of the fields and grew along with the harvest.[39]

*The Social Contract* opens with the famous proclamation—"All men are born free and equal, and everywhere they are in chains"—and ends with a call for "liberty, equality and fraternity." No one will doubt that Rousseau's claims, accurate or not, set in motion some of the profound political revolutions and intellectual claims of modernity which were inherited and furthered by people such as Le Corbusier. I would therefore agree with Vogt's argument that "LC aimed at nothing less than transposing Jean-Jacques' body of thought into the language of architecture," and that the League of Nations, like his early houses, was designed to reestablish the conditions of a Rousseauesque garden of Eden. Akin to Rousseau's conviction that democratic freedom was invested as a fundamental right in the name of man as a noble savage, Le Corbusier's project was to return, to reestablish for this reborn noble savage—embodied in the image of the upright Modulor Man—his rightful home, the rightful conditions of his being.[40]

What is of interest here, is the manner in which the evidence for the correctness of Rousseau's claim was found by Le Corbusier in the ways of living of the "primitive" uncorrupted people just then being "discovered" in the world. Le Corbusier's Rousseau lecture on the League of Nations project, on the basis of which *Precisions* was written, was delivered in Brazil. It is therefore not unexpected to find that he verifies the truth of his claims by referring to "houses of men" that have "inevitable arrangements" and that are to be found on the hills inhabited by the "blacks":

I find again in what I call the *houses of men* these inevitable arrangements. I have already explained these ideas in *Une Maison—Un Palais*. But important Brazilian personages are furious to learn that in Rio I had climbed a hill inhabited by the blacks: "It is a shame for us, civilized persons." I explained serenely that, first of all, I found these blacks basically good: good hearted. Then, beautiful, magnificent. Then, their carelessness, the limits they had learned to impose on their needs, their capacity for dreaming, their candidness resulted in their houses being always admirably sited, the windows opening astonishingly on magnificent spaces, the smallness of their rooms largely adequate.[41]

This is where Le Corbusier identifies himself as a Rousseauist:

If I think of architecture as the "houses of man," I become Rousseauist: "Man is good." And if I think of architecture as "houses of architects" I become skeptical, pessimistic. … This is what the analysis of architecture leads to, architecture being the result of the state of the mind of a period. We have come to a dead end, the social and psychological gears are disorganized. We are thirsty to be Montaigne or Rousseau undertaking a voyage to question the "naked man."[42]

Le Corbusier's "voyage to question the naked man" is identical to his search for the "houses of man" of architecture. It was the search for Rousseau's "naked man" that took him on his first *Journey to the East* (faithfully recorded in *Precisions)*[43] and that also found him in Rio "on the hill inhabited by blacks." In the nineteenth century, the habitat, morality and lifestyle—indeed, the entire culture—of the noble savage was recreated counterfactually through overzealous interpretations of archaeological and ethnological "facts." Vogt points out (although the irony seems to elude him) that during Le Corbusier's childhood, as in the colonizing imagination of Europe as a whole, the scant evidence of archaeological finds was embellished by observations of tribal and other "primitive" civilization that had newly been "discovered" by Europe. This was called the "reverse ethnological method": "'one would never have imagined this … and yet it was the case' that 'the greatest analogy' was discovered 'between our own savages on our lakes and the faraway savages on the Polynesian islands.'"[44]

Retrospectively, we can easily discern the inherent racism and acute ethnocentrism of these preposterous assertions. In the nineteenth century, however, they established the veracity of modernism's claims to being "natural" and universal, that is they literally verified them, made them into truth. Vogt reports that derivative images of the Pacific Island dwellers were printed into the textbooks of junior school when Le Corbusier was a high school student. The images and lessons he learned then seem to have stayed with him for long.

The "civilized men" warned him, Le Corbusier laughs, that the "blacks will kill you … they are extremely dangerous, they are savages." He answered: "They only kill the thief of love, he who wounded them profoundly in their flesh. Why do you want them to kill me, who look[s] at them with perfect understanding? My eyes, my smile protect me, don't worry."[45]

Le Corbusier did not worry. He was one of them, or rather one with the savages, in "perfect understanding." They spoke a common tongue that went much deeper than the superficiality of language. And what was more, Le Corbusier was also the liberating agent of modernity, self-appointed to restore their "inevitable arrangements" by his designs for the new *maisons des hommes*.

This is where we can return to the drawing of the donkey driver that Le Corbusier, communicating across the silence with "perfect understanding," had cast into concrete. Why did he do it? Le Corbusier, of course, recognized it as the work of a fellow man and wished to herald it as such. But more than that, having it cast into concrete represented the cementing of an unspoken pact. Concrete was Le Corbusier's chosen material of modernity, a material that had the "clarity of spirit" (3#277) and strength necessary for the liberation of the primitive man. Casting the donkey driver's drawing, originally made in mud, into concrete symbolically represented the liberation and transformation of that primitive man. On a larger scale, this liberation was to be enabled by the new institutions of democracy—the rightful form of governance of the man of the Enlightenment—whose rightful architectural forms were being designed in concrete by Le Corbusier. The pictures of the Indian laborers lifting loads in front of the Capitol buildings were therefore not studies in contrast, but, like the hyphen between *maison* and *palais*, were the symbols of the reestablishment of the rightful order, or rather of the claim to such a reestablishment.

The rightful use of knowledge, leading to right action, constitutes the ethical decision and promise of the Enlightenment hero battling against the improper uses of knowledge—war, destruction, greed, money. It is a question of choice, as Le Corbusier put it. The key to the Capitol's Edenic landscape, I would therefore suggest, is the tree of knowledge that occupies the center of the lower half of the Enamel Door painting. It also sets the vertical axis in the painting that is echoed by the pivot just behind it, around which the Door turns. The tree is central to the "rediscovery of man" and leads to the re-establishment of the "vertical axis of fundamental laws." The proper use of the fruits of the tree of knowledge, in other words, signifies the acts that will, in Le Corbusier's vocabulary, reestablish the vertical axis that is pivotal to the reestablishment of the proper order.

While modern civilization and "money" are the cause of man's "downfall," civilization is also the source of his salvation. Against the narcissistic desire to return to a preindustrial Eden, Le Corbusier's modernism offers a path that regains the proper conditions of man, while utilizing the causes of his downfall, industrialization, scientism, etc., by returning them to their rightful path and by scapegoating money. Le Corbusier's Capitol, his New Bethlehem, thus, does not posit a simple return to the garden of Eden. Rather, in the great western dialectical tradition, it signifies another return at a higher plain of enlightenment, achieved precisely through a prodigal journey through the plains of knowledge. (This is the modernity, the modern times that are separated by a "ditch" from the village and its pastures to "prevent confusion.")

The prodigal journey relies on, indeed requires, an image of the proper nature of man as the agent of progress. This image is given by Rousseau's "noble savage" or primitive man, the uncorrupted carrier of a millennial civilization. *In theory*, the world of the noble savage is the idyllic world of Eden, a bucolic symphony regained, rediscovered and reestablished on earth, a relationship of brotherhood between the cosmos and living things: stars, nature, sacred animals, birds, monkeys, and cows, and in the village, children, adults and old people, and the pond form a harmonious unity.

*In practice*, however, the conditions that verify, that literally make into truth this claim, have yet to be established, have yet to be made evident, since the improper uses of knowledge result in the alienation of man. Indeed this work of verifying the "truth" is the critical task of the modern subject and the Enlightenment hero of rediscovering "man" and the "straight line wedding the axis of fundamental laws."

In this way, the reestablishment of the natural home of man as a secularized Eden initiates an apocalyptic journey that reinstates the conditions of the Judeo-Christian-Islamic paradigm that promises the recovery of the lost fullness of Adam's true home. The verification of the "truth" of the noble savage, in other words, resumes the structure of the Judeo-Christian-Islamic eschatology where salvation tomorrow is a promise based on an image of a lost but recoverable yesterday, and relies on the morality of the work done today.[46]

Therefore, one can venture, Le Corbusier is projecting onto the poor villagers of the Capitol the role of primitive man, of the noble savage, Adam reconciled with his original home in Eden. This fantasy is enabled and empowered by its inscription as a prophetic event in Le Corbusier's conception of his own destiny as tied to modernism's apocalyptic mission. In this context, the poor village peasants with their millennial world are not only the favored subjects who are promised fulfillment in the Second Machine Age, but the future industrial revolution that Le Corbusier hoped was to come, and which would be driven not by the profit motive but by the egalitarian principle of providing sufficient material goods for all. Even more importantly, it is their presence—the fact that they exist—that enables Le Corbusier to justify and verify his own sense of self and modernism's promise of fulfilling the ideal of the noble savage. They are, in other words, critical to the prophetic purpose of modernism; they are its subjects.

There are thus some grounds for understanding why Le Corbusier founded the entire Capitol around them—without any exchange and without them ever having commissioned him to do so. Labeled a "futuristic thinker," Le Corbusier, in his own personal world, interpreted his commission as a recognition of his messianic mission. But he must have been aware that what was expected of him as a "futurist" was to be a technologist-transformer, a standard-bearer of the progress of the West. Consequently, he masked his personal agenda behind this misplaced expectation—this misrecognition, as it were—as a subtext visible only to the initiated. The camouflage, though thick, is decipherable.

# The Aesthetics of the High Court and the Assembly

When he joined the Capital project, my father was the "juniormost of the junior architects." The senior architects were Pierre Jeanneret, Maxwell Fry, and Jane Drew. The junior architects were the team of nine Indian architects and planners hired to assist the seniors. These were—in the bureaucratic order of seniority—M. N. Sharma, A. R. Prabhawalkar, B. P. Mathur, Piloo Moody, U. E. Chowdhury, N. S. Lamba, Jeet Lal Malhotra, J. S. Dethe, and Aditya Prakash (fig. 4.1).

The junior architects were considered as trainees being groomed for the job of building the future cities of modern India. This was not easy, a matter not just of professional practice but of the enormous psychological task of learning an idiom, weighted with authority, one term at a time:

> When I [Aditya Prakash] joined, everyone called me the juniormost junior architect. I did not respond. In the evening we used to go for a walk. Near the bus-stand there used to be an old village pond. The trunk of a tree lay there projecting over the pond. I used to sit on it a little away from any other company. I believe I would be contemplating the nature or something. I did not talk much. I was yet not familiar with the Corbusier systems. Persons like Prabhawalkar and Jeet Lal Malhotra were full of Corbusier. B. P. Mathur was the favourite of Maxwell Fry. They talked about MODULOR and Zoning and CIAM Grid, and the rule of the Vs—all terms being quite strange to me. I found myself quite inadequate for the job. When I responded to something I gave a rather enigmatic smile which was dubbed as the million dollar smile of Mona Lisa.
>
> But I can say to my credit that I was a quick learner. I soon picked up the ropes and familiarized myself with all the terms and their significance. I did not hesitate to ask if I did not understand something…[In time] I had gained enough confidence and I was asked to PRESENT Chandigarh to [visitors]. In fact most of the time it was my privilege to EXPLAIN. Perhaps I could do so better than anybody else. Hugh Casson and Kwame N'Krumah also visited, then many younger architects from all over the world would come to feel the ambience of the growing city. They would stay for a few days and go quite happy.[1]

Retrospectively, it is not so difficult for a historian to "explain" the gridded Master Plan of Chandigarh. Le Corbusier insistently drilled its concepts into every publication on the city, and what was once obfuscated cabalism is now everyday

**Fig. 4.1** The complete team of the Capitol Project, photographed in front of their temporary office.

gospel. Most architecture students, in India as around the world, can easily summarize the hierarchy of the urban plan—the circulation system, the sectors, and the neighborhood unit.

Perhaps it is understood much too well, for it is the urban character of the city that has come under the severest criticism. In a recent conference in 1999, "Celebrating 50 years of Chandigarh," Charles Correa notoriously dubbed it a "zenana" city—a women's city, protected for the weak and precious few, cloistered and enclosed. At this conference, dedicated to reassessing the city, numerous visiting architects, planners, and historians offered their own visions and re-visions of the Master Plan.

Few, however, questioned the Capitol buildings. They all seemed to be sold on the aesthetic brilliance of Le Corbusier's architecture, if not his urban planning. The Chandigarh administration, the official hosts of the conference, even had a full-size façade of the unbuilt Governor's Palace mocked up to envision what the Capitol would look like with it. Happy with the results, calls were made to have the Governor's Palace constructed. The hat was passed around. And the motion was even floated to declare the Capitol complex a "World Heritage Site." The motion did not pass. It was ironic, however, that the Capitol, that unbridled essay in modernism, was already ready for the rubbish heap of history!

What are the Capitol buildings really about? Always forthcoming with his views on planning, Le Corbusier never offered explanations for his architecture. "The

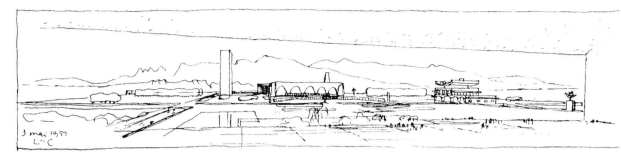

**Fig. 4.2** Le Corbusier's earliest sketch of the Capitol Complex.

artist never tells!" Perhaps that is why his architecture at least is still revered in some quarters. But for the postcolonial historian, *explaining* it is a matter of pride. Explaining Chandigarh, explaining the Capitol, demystifying its content, removing it from the hallowed pedestal of obscurity, familiarizing it and making it one's own, enables the postcolonial architect—and intellectual—to gain confidence, to prepare the ground to speak with a voice of one's own.

*The word "appearance" still languishes in the shadow of Plato's disdain.*
—*Robin Evans*

### For the Mind's Pleasure: Architectural Artifice

Caroline Constant has suggested that the Capitol should first and foremost be considered as a landscape project.[2] Her suggestion, I think, is very important, because the Capitol buildings, bound in from the south by the artificial hills and from the north by the not so distant Himalayas, inhabit their site through a visible relationship, a juxtaposition that is drawn against and into the landscape. Most of Le Corbusier's sketches draw the Capitol buildings into a vast plain, always framed against the dramatic Himalayan silhouette (fig. 4.2). There is a sense in these sketches, from the very first that Le Corbusier did when he reached the site, that the buildings manifest their presence through a juxtaposition of appearances—*when measured against the Himalayas.* In a short but enlightening discussion of the Capitol in his book on proportions, *The Modulor*, Le Corbusier writes: "We are in a plain, the chain of the Himalayas locks the landscape magnificently to the north. The smallest building appears tall and commanding"[3] (plate 9).

Appearances, in other words, were critical to the composition of the Capitol. It is not surprising, therefore, to find that Le Corbusier used sketches drawn on site to make critical design decisions. Determining the exact location of the buildings on site, determining appearances, in Le Corbusier's highly personalized aesthetic vocabulary was "a question of optics":

The question of optics became paramount when we had to decide where to put the government buildings. … We made some masts, eight meters high, painted alternately black and white, each bearing a white flag. We tried, for the first time to apportion the site. The corners of the Palaces were fixed by black and white masts. It was found that the intervals between buildings were too large.[4]

As Le Corbusier stood on the Esplanade in the middle of the Capitol to "apportion the site," Indian workmen in the distance held up survey rods, painted black and white, to help him make his judgments. The survey rods, with their carriers, were located to outline the proposed positions of the Capitol buildings. With these rods as guides, Le Corbusier quickly drew the buildings from his eye level. When the "intervals" were too large, or too small, he had the masts moved and then redrew, again and again, until he was satisfied with the composition (figs. 4.3, 4.4). (2#742-3)

"Sur place = exact"—"on place = exact" is the annotation on the sketch the Le Corbusier drew to record the final position of the Capitol buildings (plate 5). (2#722-3) This sketch is accompanied by a quick plan with a cross-axis drawn onto it, locking the

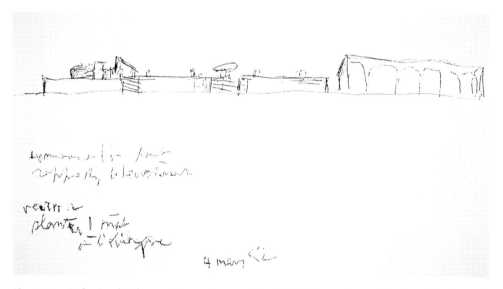

Fig. 4.3. Le Corbusier sketch examining various positions for the Secretariat and the Assembly. (2#742)

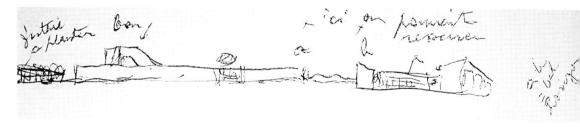

Fig. 4.4. Le Corbusier sketch examining various positions for the Secretariat and the Assembly. (2#743)

Capitol buildings in relation to each other.[5] Since the exactness of the sketch refers to the visual harmony of the buildings and their landscape, the cross-axis in the plan, it follows, documents that decision, that visual observation in plan. Or so it seems from the sketch.[6]

The fact that this "question of optics" played such a significant role in determining the final location of the Capitol buildings would be rather unremarkable were it not for the fact that it contradicts a very precise claim that Le Corbusier makes for the plan of the Capitol. In his article "The Master Plan," this is how Le Corbusier describes the mathematics of this idealized plan:

> Four obelisks (or any other shape) shall determine in the heart of nature, the angles of a square of 800 meters: four others shall determine the square of 400 meters containing the Secretariat and Assembly buildings and the "Museum of Knowledge." The High Court palace occupies the second square of 400 at the East.[7]

Although from this description the plan appears to be ascertained by geometrical certainties, it is not very clear how these squares in fact "contain" the buildings, or how the High Court "occupies" its 400-meter square. If one triangulates the squares to ascertain their geometries, it is readily apparent that they do so, if at all, only very approximately. The Assembly is just about in the middle of the western 400-meter square, and the Secretariat and the Museum of Knowledge are at its edge. On the other side, the High Court is just beyond the center of its square. In a framework of such precision, these are gross approximations.

Greater insight into the manner in which this containment and occupation might take place can be gained in the discussion of the same question in *The Modulor*. The squares it seems here, are not geometric, but "arithmetic," determining entities, "conjugating" buildings in their ratios:

> The government buildings are conjugated with one another in a strict ratio of heights and sizes. For the mind's pleasure, it was decided to manifest this fundamental arithmetic by putting up obelisks; a first series would mark the 800-metre square, a second the 400-metre squares. The first would be erected out in the country, the second close to the buildings, forming part in the composition.[8]

Conjugation, as in the rules of grammar, implies a product that issues as a consequence of the observation of prescribed rules. *The Modulor*, from which these quotes are taken, was Le Corbusier's rule book, a system of proportioning produced by intuitively interlocking mathematical and geometric equivalences—the golden ratio and the right angle—and a governing height based on a six-foot "Modulor Man."[9] Le Corbusier ascribed an occult power to mathematical relations and considered them keys to esoteric knowledge, accessible only to the initiated. The 1:1.6 approximations of the Fibbonaci series fascinated him. His aspiration was that the *Modulor* would disclose a visual scale similar to the harmonic scale in music, so that its "arithmetic," or its "conjugations," could be harmonized into an optical music as it were.

Although geometry was fundamental to their derivation, the relationships among the *Modulor* dimensions are not visible, as one might expect, through obvious geometric relationships such as axes and parallelism. Rather, they visually relate only as a set of dimensions that can be variously assembled to add up to each other. Used out of sequence, however, their primary relationships can only be intuited, presumably as one intuits the underlying presence of the harmonic scale in a musical composition. This is what made them in Le Corbusier's eyes arithmetic and harmonic. He called them *les traces regulateurs*.

All the dimensions of the Chandigarh Capitol were derived from the *Modulor*; Le Corbusier described it as the only "luxury" that was used to design Chandigarh.[10] One might surmise, therefore, that in the *Modulor* compositions, the Capitol squares functioned as *traces regulateurs*—regulating lines that intelligibly underlie the composition, and not the determining geometries of visual or planar axes—conjugating the Capitol buildings into harmonic relationships. In fact, if one traces a golden section arc through the 400-meter square on the right, one can locate the position of the High Court (fig. 4.5). If one looks further, one could find a whole series of similar underlying "harmonic" relationships, as if the whole composition were something of a symphony.

This, however, still does not fully explain the "question of optics" that Le Corbusier so critically drew into his sketchbook, standing in the middle of the Capitol plain, measuring the survey rods. Sketching buildings into place is not a precise geometric or arithmetic operation. Yet, in Le Corbusier's aesthetic world, these activities are

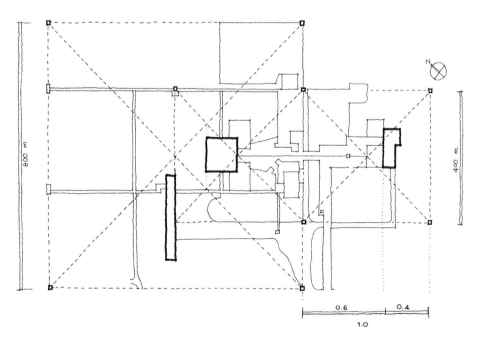

Fig. 4.5. The golden section (0.6 : 0.4) in the plan of the Capitol complex locates the front of the High Court in one of the 400-meter squares. (Drawing by Kanog-Anong Nimakorn)

interrelated. Indeed, he not only ascribes great import to that act of sketching, but in fact adduces it as the critical "truth" of the process of making design decisions. Here it is in *The Modulor*:

> There was anxiety and anguish in taking decisions on that vast, limitless ground. A pathetic soliloquy! I had to appreciate and to decide alone. The problem was no longer one of reasoning but of sensation. Chandigarh is not a city of lords, princes or kings confined within walls, crowded in by neighbors. It was a matter of occupying a plain. *The geometrical event was, in truth, a sculpture of the intellect.* No potter's clay in your hands to experiment with. No maquette that could ever have served as a genuine aid to a decision. It was a tension, mathematical in nature, which would bear fruit only when the buildings were completed. The right point. The right distance. Appreciation. Groping, we brought the masts closer to one another. It was a battle of space fought within the mind.[11]

"A battle of space fought within the mind," groping, unknown, is certainly "a sculpture of the intellect." Yet, in the above passage this "sculpture of the intellect" is adduced as the "truth" of the geometrical event; sensation is produced as the truth of reasoning, and, by extension I would suggest, anguish and anxiety are produced as the nature of certainty and singularity.

How does a geometric event "in truth" become a sculpture of the intellect? How do the geometric and the visual events lay claim to the same landscape? How does the plan become the sketch? Or is it vice versa? In the section preceding the one I quoted just above, Le Corbusier describes the process as something magical—an architectural artifice:

> Arithmetic: arithmetic lends itself to a simple operation of the mind. Twice two is four. It is palpable, comprehensible (I have not said 'visible'). … it is natural, useful and pleasant to give [the Capitol] … a geometrical shape, once again palpable and intelligent. But, by an architectural artifice, the ideas will pass from the 'conceivable' to the 'visible.' Here is how it is done; a first diagram of two 800 meter squares. …[12]

The conceivable, the plan, thus passes into the visible, the actual building, by an architectural artifice. The artifice—the problem of sensation—quite clearly is executed in the sketching, a connection that has been veiled, probably quite intentionally, by Le Corbusier. And yet the publication of the artifice's existence and the centrality of its claim begs interpretation; it is after all "the truth." What is the artifice? How is it conceived? What does it conceive?

Artifice by definition is hidden; like a building's foundation, it functions precisely when it is buried, unseen. Otherwise it is just method. The paradoxical job of the theorist, if one does not believe in magic or theology, is to speculate on its properties, to propel a sonar in search of resonant sounds. "Acoustic," "ineffable," "plastic"—Le Corbusier used numerous terms to convey the unconveyability of his artifice. In the following, I weave some of my own interpretive studies, drawing as much from Freudian psychoanalysis as from careful observation, into threads from Le Corbusier's work. The blurry but perceptible picture that emerges, simulates the experiencing—the question of sensation—of the Capitol buildings, primarily the High Court and the Assembly.

## First Plan: The (Uncanny) Aesthetic of the High Court

*Truly the key to my artistic creation is my pictorial work, begun in 1918 and pursued regularly each day. The foundation of my research and intellectual production has its secret in the uninterrupted practice of my painting. It is there that one must find the source of my spiritual freedom, of my disinterestedness, of the faithfulness and the integrity of my work.*

*—Le Corbusier*

Sites of immense aesthetic struggle, the designs of the Capitol buildings underwent numerous revisions in the process of metamorphosizing into their final form and order. As they stand, the Capitol buildings, especially the Assembly, betray the stress marks of these efforts and their ambitious aesthetic expectations. As noted in chapter 2,

Fig. 4.6. Le Corbusier sketch of the Capitol Complex against the Himalayas.

somewhere between June and December 1951, very soon after Le Corbusier's first visit and sketch of the Capitol, the Secretariat changed from being a vertical structure to a horizontal one, and the Capitol itself was redirected from being the visible head of the city to being a self-enclosed world. Besides its political and intellectual implications, this change was ultimately echoed in the designs of the capitol buildings, reorienting their collective focus.

To begin at the beginning. The earliest drawings Le Corbusier published in the volumes of the *Œuvre complète* in 1953 focus on the long expanse of the horizon line. These first sketches show the buildings as mere specks, juxtaposed with the animals and mango trees, etched against a distant horizon (fig. 4.6). The visual focus is clearly on the Secretariat and the Governor's Palace. These are composed as upward thrusting counterpoints to the horizon and the general horizontality of the Capitol; the former with its solid vertical mass and the latter with its sweeping, sky-turned parasol roof (fig. 2.7). After it was laid flat, the Secretariat added to the long horizontality of the general schema (fig. 2.8), and although it still contributed significantly to the composition with its size and roofline, after this change the Governor's Palace became the singular visual focus of the Capitol.

The High Court and the Assembly, in both these proposals of 1951, function like flanking twins working in concordance, choreographed for harmonic effect. Their main facades, directly facing each other across the central esplanade, are very similar, dominated by gigantic orders of arches, with deep, dramatic shadows. Like aisles framing the altar, these twins have as their focus, and clearly defer to, the Governor's Palace, which is in the center of the composition. In the limelight, framed against the Himalayas, the Governor's Palace is the culmination of this dramatic and self-assured composition, gathering the surroundings, including the sky, into its acoustic curves.

Indeed, it is evident that Le Corbusier went to significant lengths to ensure that the visual hierarchy between the Governor's Palace and its subsidiaries was suitably staged. Although the High Court in section has the same dramatic inverted parasol profile as the Governor's Palace, Le Corbusier deliberately masked it by an overextended parapet wall along its shorter elevation. Along the longer facade he hung false, decorative arches that make it seem like they support the parasol roof, rather than vice versa. This masking of the section is so complete and so successful, that if one compares the section with its elevations, it is difficult at first glance to correlate them, even with a trained eye (figs. 4.7, 4.8). A simple rectilinear box on the outside, the High Court hides a flashy section with careful deliberation.

There is, however, method to the madness. Other than making sure that it does not visually compete with the Governor's Palace, the High Court, the first of the Capitol buildings to be completed, the one that was most faithful to the earliest impulses of the design, has an aesthetic syntax of its own. It is less eye-catching than that of the Governor's Palace—except in peripheral vision. It requires the suspension of visual disbelief.

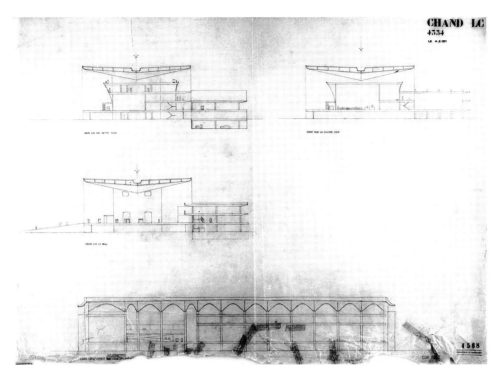

Fig. 4.7. Front elevation and three sections of the High Court.

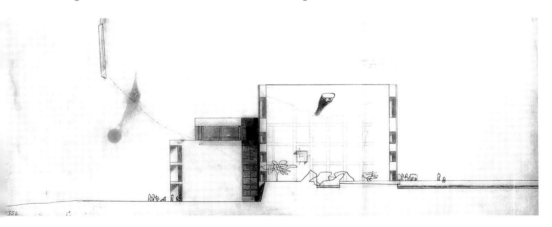

Fig. 4.8. Side elevation of the High Court with masked section drawn in.

Our initial clues again lie in painting. Soon after he started painting in 1918, Le Corbusier lost and never regained sight in one eye. One can speculate that, bereft of three-dimensional perception, painting not only enabled him to study visual relationships among forms, but also was a means of examining their three-dimensional interrelationships on a two-dimensional surface. Cubist painting technique is founded on such an examining of three-dimensional properties of the world in a two-dimensional medium, and Le Corbusier's purist paintings, based on cubism and done early in his career, are particularly interesting in this regard. Like cubist paintings, they interrelate the second and the third dimensions, different only in so far as Le Corbusier used everyday objects like bottles and cups and painted them with exactitude.[13] Something like free-associative orthogonal architectural drawings, these paintings juxtapose plan with elevation, along with impressions of shade and shadow, forming complex, multi-layered plays in optical relationships.

Later in life, Le Corbusier was more free in his formal compositions, but it seems that some old purist memories may have returned transformed when he set out to design the Capitol. In the High Court, the purist play with forms is itself played with. If purist paintings disclose and examine the disjuncture between plan and elevation, the plan and elevation of the High Court, in apparent parody, are doubles of each other. If one removes the arches, one discovers that the bays of the courtrooms, with their entrance portal and supporting corridor, are mirrored in the elevation.[14] They are, in other

Fig. 4.9. Photo and Le Corbusier sketches of the High Court with water reflections. (From Le Corbusier [c. 1950–60], p. 183)

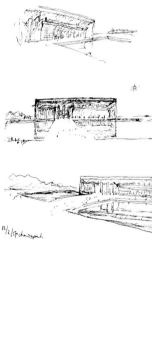

Le portique de la Haute-Cour

words, reflections of each other, and together they form a horizontally symmetrical composition.

   This horizontal reflective symmetry itself has a double. The elevation is also mirrored in the reflecting pools at the High Court's base, which not only doubles the apparent size of the building (when measured against the Himalayas) but also gives the composition an uncanny surreal spin. If in one's mind's eye one draws a horizontal axis at the base of the High Court elevation, one can literally "spin" the building around that axis—from the elevation, down to the plan, and underneath upside down through the reflection, and back up … (figs. 4.9, 4.10). In the mind's eye, when one stands on site and experiences this, given the enormous size of the High Court, the effect can be dizzying.

   This spinning effect is emphasized by the thick frame that encircles the High Court. In most photographs, and in so many of Le Corbusier's sketches, it is this frame that swings around in its reflection, encircling and framing a picture that appears to be suspended in space (fig. 4.9). An important consequence of this is that the access path from the Capitol Esplanade appears to enter the High Court in the *middle* of the composition.[15] Surrounded by water on two sides, this path becomes a bridge that is suspended in midair, abstracted from the ground plane. Strangely derealized and

Fig. 4.10. Analytic drawings showing how the High Court "spins" around its axis.
(Drawing by Kanog-Anong Nimakorn)

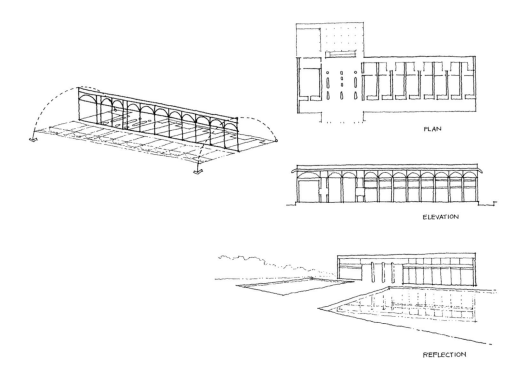

PLAN

ELEVATION

REFLECTION

uncanny, liberated of its gravitational obligations, the High Court, in peripheral vision, appears indeed to be weightless.[16]

To summarize the artifice then, the High Court's aesthetic composition is designed not only to carefully mask its section but to insinuate a set of horizontal symmetries through a subtle play of appearances. As a consequence, the downward crushing, familiar density of weight is neutralized, de-familiarized and rendered weightless, at least in peripheral vision. Le Corbusier never ceased to pontificate that architecture was heavy and regulated by the laws of physics—"It's good that the fools take their turn to speak, because we others might forget the weight of stones and the sweat necessary to move them."[17] The High Court, however, both reaffirms and challenges this claim. It is a mask of mirrors, an intellectual sculpture of the mind, energized by sensation.

Now, symmetries have always held sway in aesthetic compositions; but the weightlessness of the High Court's horizontal symmetry (versus the groundedness of vertical symmetry) is exceptional and provocative. In an article entitled "Mies van der Rohe's Paradoxical Symmetries," architectural historian and theorist Robin Evans notes the presence of similar horizontal symmetries in the Bauhaus modernist Ludwig Mies van der Rohe's 1929 German Pavilion at the World Fair in Barcelona, Spain.[18] Besides being doubled in reflection ponds, Mies's Pavilion is also horizontally symmetrical at the eye level—an effect of the height of the building being twice the human eye level, the horizontal division of its travertine wall into two equal parts, and the reflective nature of the ceiling and floor. Evans notes that he was often confused about the correct orientation of his slides, which alerted him to this horizontal symmetry.

One is habitually familiar and comfortable with vertical symmetry, for it reflects the composition of the human body, which helps ground oneself when experiencing it. Conversely, horizontal symmetry in architecture, Evans points out, tends to keep the viewer floating in suspension, against the laws of gravity, even if only subliminally. This can be a destabilizing experience, for one always presumes buildings to be weighed down by gravity. The consequence is that in the thrall of horizontal symmetry, while experiencing a building normally, the viewer is subject to a sublime and subliminal levitational experience. It promotes an aesthetic suspension of disbelief inducing a momentary distraction from one's natural and familiar contexts and conditions of perception, i.e., from reality.

In other words, horizontal symmetry impregnates the familiar gravitational grounding of architecture with an ungrounded, abstracted, and derealized subtext. The sensory effect of weightlessness as the defiance of gravity is, of course, a familiar aesthetic trope, as provoked, for instance, by the dizzying heights of the gothic cathedral or the unbelievable span of a grand dome. What is particular about the effect of weightlessness created by horizontal symmetry, when it works well, is that it acts subliminally, countervailing and canceling the normative expectations of the purposes of architecture. The subliminal character of the effect renders the experience of the entire composition simultaneously familiar and unfamiliar. Subliminal suggestions merge into their overt pre-texts, and *it is their productive interference*, like that of sound waves, that generates the complete aesthetic experience. The familiar indeed becomes unfamiliar in a sudden rush of realization in the peripheral vision of the mind's eye. This is a quietly ethereal, anxiety provoking, and yet fascinating and magical experience.

An interpretation drawn from psychoanalysis can be useful here. The subtextual residence of the unfamiliar within the home of the familiar describes the operations of the uncanny. Always connected with some form of doubling, the uncanny, as theorized by Sigmund Freud, is characterized by a sense of anxiety that is a consequence of an unintended and unexpected repetition.[19] It is an aesthetic effect that is, as Freud put it:

> often and easily produced when the distinction between imagination and reality is effaced, as when something that we have hitherto regarded as imaginary appears before us in reality, or when a symbol takes over the full function of the thing it symbolizes, and so on. It is this factor which contributes not a little to the uncanny effect attaching to magical practices.[20]

Repetition that erases the distinction between the imaginary and the real is an artifice that defamiliarizes the familiar, that produces the magical and ethereal effect of the uncanny. As such it is an aesthetic experience that is cathectic rather than cathartic.[21] A cathectic experience induces an aesthetic response that, rather than resulting in an emotional release like catharsis, imbues the experiencer with an excess of unresolved emotional energy, provoking an unnerving semi-ecstatic anxiety. It is liberating only in the same paradoxical way that loss of control is.

Le Corbusier once scribbled in his sketchbook: "'analysis' (which is what 'Engineers' do) results in 'psychic security'. But 'synthesis' (which is what 'Architects' do) results in 'anxiety.'" (3#203)

The same "anxiety" was encountered on the Capitol plain, in the quote that I referred to earlier: "There was anxiety and anguish in taking decisions on that vast, limitless ground. A pathetic soliloquy! I had to appreciate and to decide alone. The problem was no longer one of reasoning but of sensation."[22]

Decisions become a problem of sensation. The Chandigarh Capitol, from the human eye level, is indeed vast and limitless. Dimensioned against the Himalayas, it stretches into the distance. In these expanses, the Capitol buildings have to struggle to generate any sense of enclosure that is comprehensible on the scale of the human body. This is precisely what the Capitol has often been criticized for. And yet, it was at the same human eye level, with survey rods staffed by Indian workmen in the distance, that Le Corbusier made his decisions. And his justification was aesthetic, he made them a "problem of sensation." The reason why the dimensions of the Capitol are difficult to grasp, I would therefore suggest, is because they do not belong to the more quotidian frameworks of order. Their aesthetic logic is imbued with the uncanny.

According to Freud, the experience of the uncanny is associated with the return of the repressed—a recurrence or remembering of a past in an unexpected and displaced forum. This remembering, however, reconstructs that past not through the reclaiming of a lost account but by means of the affective production of a fantasy, which presents itself *as if* recovered from the past. Here one can recall Vogt's provocative thesis that Le Corbusier's pilotis is based on the attempt to recover the primordial life of "stilt dwelling people," whose remains were supposedly discovered on Switzerland's Lac Léman. Vogt suggests that Le Corbusier deeply internalized these discoveries (that were written about in his high school text books) and that the location of the pilotis that hold up the head of his League of Nations Project right at the edge of Lac Léman recreates the situation of the stilt dwellings.[23]

Whether or not Le Corbusier consciously or unconsciously continued to believe in the veracity of the accounts about these stilt dwellings, it is still possible that the Capitol and its protracted play on reflective symmetries may also have its origins in a lost memory of the stilt dwellings, not of the stilts themselves but of the entire lake. The vast but bound expanse of the Capitol plain may be a transformed repetition of the surface of the lake, literally turned into stone. One does literally float on a lake, a state that is reproduced on the Capitol by the sensation of weightlessness. How can one architecturally occupy a vast plain? What if it were conceived as a lake, bound all around, a presence in and of itself, framing a structure or two? One can also note that the Secretariat, when seen on edge from the south, does appear like a vast ocean liner, ploughing its way through a sea of green.[24]

There is, of course, a "real" lake just to the east of the Capitol, but Le Corbusier chose not to build directly on it, or at its edge.[25] Perhaps that might have been much too close. But he did not hesitate to record his admiration of the Capitol when viewed from the Lake:

> Moving through the space between the lake (the dam) and the Capitol … I discover Asiatic Space. My palaces 1500 meters away fill the horizon better than at 650 meters. … The scale is more noble and grand from a distance.[26] From the High Court, the Secretariat is too close. It is handsome but it is full of grandeur from over there, in the midst of the countryside and cultivated fields. (4#13)

More noble and grand from a distance? How could the High Court and the Secretariat, that have always been criticized for being too far, especially if one has to walk the 650 meters from one to the other in India's hot summer sun, be too close? The Capitol is a surreal landscape. Le Corbusier measured it against the mountains. To grasp this measurement, one needs, I would suggest, to float somewhat in the absurd and subliminal play of appearances (figs. 4.9, 4.11; plate 10). (3#606)

Fig. 4.11. Le Corbusier's sketch of the Capitol from the Lake. (3#606)

### Second Plan: The Prophetic Transformation of the Assembly Building

When the artist has to make decisions, he does not hesitate, Le Corbusier often said, because he has prepared to make that decision for a long time. It was his "law of the meander": the moment of insight, when it discloses itself, will be grasped by the creative hand if it has been prepared to accept it.[27] But Le Corbusier was also superstitious. One of his better-known Indian collaborators and disciples, Balkrishna Doshi, notes that Le Corbusier always carried a particular coin with him that constantly burned a hole in his pocket.[28] The unexpected appearance of things, like prophetic stars in the sky, held profound significance for him.

One of the best recorded "appearances" in Chandigarh, again an uncanny doubling, is the birth in 1952 of the *Taureaux* series of gouaches. Le Corbusier records that on 26 April 1952, above the plains of Chandigarh, a sketch of one of his old purist paintings that happened to be turned at ninety degrees, stirred a new discovery in him. "One fine day the discovery of a bull on my canvases came to light, quite out of my control," Le Corbusier wrote to a collector years later.[29] Page 232 of his *Creation Is a Patient Search* documents the event graphically. Le Corbusier had a photograph of his painting "Still Life" with him—a painting playing on the typical cubist/purist themes of

Fig. 4.12 Le Corbusier's sketch of the origin of the *Taureaux* series.

doubling and displacement.[30] The painting has a horizontal aspect ratio, but Le Corbusier sketched it vertically extracting and reformatting forms to cull together a bull figure[31] (fig. 4.12).

Le Corbusier became obsessed with this bull, and the *Taureaux* series of paintings dominated the last years of his life. While he was working on four to five paintings at the same time, slowly a host of other themes, particularly those of the female body, were merged into the paintings. The aspect ratio of the paintings themselves changed from being vertical to horizontal, but the important point was that it was the first rotation of the painting that engendered new possibilities that had hitherto been hidden, "quite out of my control." Le Corbusier remained obsessed with the idea that a simple reorientation had disclosed a new truth, that something that had always been latent was finally revealed through an accident.

Again an *uncanny* doubling, a repetition with change in other words, was the fount of creation, the artifice. Jaime Coll, in his essay on Le Corbusier's paintings, notes that such rotations are analogous (and may indeed be related) to techniques such as *"bassesse,"* developed by George Braque in the late 1920s, "in which the 'formless' is 'discovered' through an axial rotation of the characteristically upright stance of the human being into the horizontal position of animals."[32] One can think of Duchamp, Picasso, and numerous other possible sources that surely went into Le Corbusier's aesthetic cauldron. One need not deny any; but what is of interest for us here is that for Le Corbusier, exhilarated by the rush of a discovery, this event had prophetic significance and, indeed, was fundamentally connected with India and with his being in India. Le Corbusier preserved this superstition. Retrospectively, he recalled, "under the sign of the bull," "all of a sudden I think about it. I began the *Taureaux* Gouaches at Chandigarh … India has lived under the sign of the Bull." (3#391)

India's living "under the sign of the Bull" may refer to the statue of the *Nandi* bull, which is always found outside a temple of Shiva and which Le Corbusier may have seen. It may also be connected to seals from the ancient Indus Valley civilization, at least one of which contained the impression of a bull, which Le Corbusier had copied for later use. But mainly the bull was preponderant in the form of the animal itself—on the plains of Chandigarh as all over the country, in the fields and villages everywhere. The family of the cow is venerated in the Hindu cosmogony, and Le Corbusier constantly drew the animals in aesthetic fascination. They appear right away with the first sketches of Chandigarh, much before and well after the "discovery" of the *Taureaux* series (fig. 4.13).

In the last quotation, Le Corbusier could simply have been exploring the ways in which impressions of India—born from his having traveled in India and having drawn it extensively—may have made their way into the unconscious aesthetic palimpsests of his mind. He rotated objects and drawings in the process of design all the time; it was one of his aesthetic processes. However, I would argue that for Le Corbusier aesthetic processes were not ends in themselves, but means to discovering the higher orders of "truth." That the discovery of a significant development in his aesthetic was made in India

Fig. 4.13. Le Corbusier's sketches of bulls in Chandigarh. (From Le Corbusier 1965, p. 71)

was therefore of prophetic significance and had somehow to be connected with his work there, as if "India, that profound and humane civilization," had spoken to him.

Ultimately, the *Taureaux* discovery had a direct impact on the design of the Assembly.[33] Early on, Le Corbusier thought of the Assembly simply as a problem involving the design of two large auditoriums. Drawings of September 1951 show studies of various possible auditorium arrangements in plan. These are accompanied by sections designed with optimum acoustic properties, as in any theater (fig. 4.14). (22#109#288) The earliest complete section, however, shows the Assembly as a large, simple cuboid in which

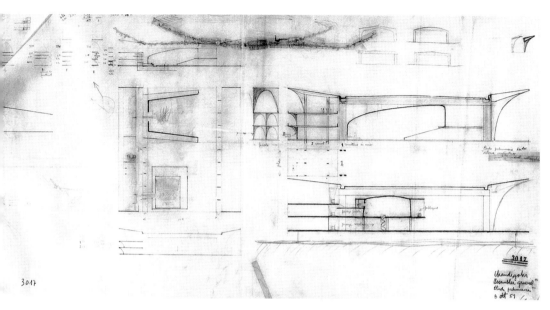

Fig. 4.14. Plan and section sketches of the Assembly in October 1951, the main chamber buried within the building as an auditorium.

the two chambers have been immersed as trapezoidal auditoriums without any acoustic considerations. The first completed design shows the cuboid flanked by two wings. One of these wings forms the entrance portal and the other a triple-story office space.

Two weeks later the first set of presentation drawings of the first fully worked-out design was complete. In the interior the two trapezoids have been converted into ovoids in plan, but their section is the same. On the exterior the entrance portal consists of five arched bays that support a projecting overhang, which, in section, looks like an aircraft's wing. The office-side facade looks very similar to the main facade of the High Court—three levels of brise-soleil separated by an entrance portal and surmounted by an arched parasol roof (which in section looks like the section of the roof over the open air altar of Le Corbusier's chapel at Ronchamp, France).[34] (22#172#3016, 22#175#3019, 22#174#3020)

At this stage, as noted, the Assembly is conceived in the same aesthetic language as the High Court. Indeed, their side elevations reveal their kinship; if the blank side facade of the High Court were split in the middle and expanded to accommodate a huge box, the High Court would become the Assembly (fig. 4.15). Since the two internal assembly chambers are almost entirely hidden, the dominant expression of the portico at this point is that of the arches of the High Court. Like the High Court, the Assembly still is horizontally symmetrical, with its own reflecting pool.

All this changed after the *Taureaux* discovery. For years the Assembly chamber had been nothing more than a large auditorium with a skylight, and Le Corbusier had concentrated on the affective performance of the eastern and western facades of the building. Admitting light from the roof was nothing more than an issue of practicality, not

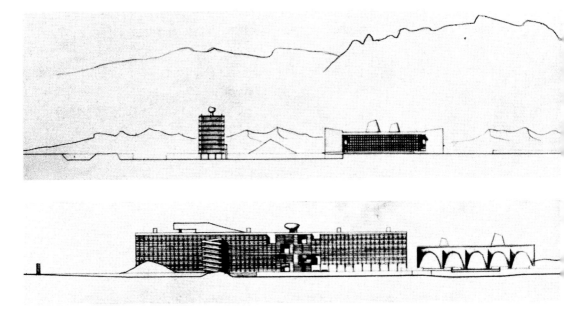

Fig. 4.15. Long elevations of the Capitol showing the relationship between the elevations of the Assembly and the High Court (closely related) and the Governor's Palace (focus of the composition). (From Le Corbusier 1953, p. 124)

a decision of exceptional symbolic significance. In June 1953, one year after the *Taureaux* discovery, Le Corbusier was in Ahmedabad, India, and on his way to the airport he saw the hyperbolic paraboloid cooling towers of a newly constructed thermal power station. Balkrishna Doshi reports that Le Corbusier stopped the car and walked into one of the towers and proceeded to clap wooden boards in various places to test its acoustics.[35] Right there and then, he decided to incorporate the tower into the Assembly. His decision was instantaneous and did not need reflection. Later, on 19 June 1953 in Bombay, he made a sketch to simply record the fact[36] (fig. 4.16).

The next set of drawings of the Capitol record that the hyperbolic paraboloid tower is incorporated into the Assembly and made into the larger of the two chambers, with the smaller one being capped by a pyramid. In the sequential development of the Assembly, the incorporation of the hyperbolic paraboloid is sudden, almost violent, and somewhat hilarious. Originally nothing more than two acoustic auditoria, the assembly chambers became ovoids with special skylights, barely contained by their enclosure. And then suddenly they burst forth from the roof, become perfect circles in plan, and dominate the formal assemblage of the Assembly.[37] The perverse humor lies in the sense that they grow like a pregnancy that suddenly erupts through the stomach when it can no longer be denied. (22#179#3025, 22#183#3032)

This event was accompanied by innumerable study drawings attempting to find ways of drawing in light from the parabolic roof so that it would form rays of light that like a large symbolic sundial would fall on significant objects within the Assembly on

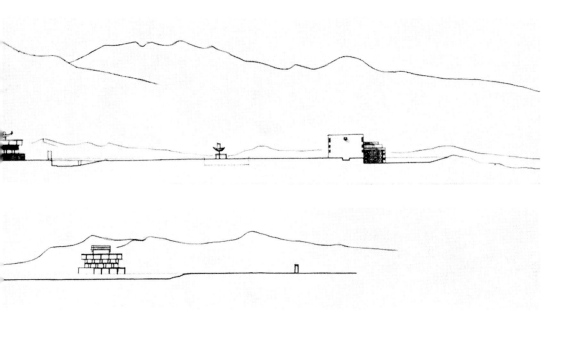

Fig. 4.16. Le Corbusier's sketch of the Assembly's section with the cooling towers in Ahmedabad.
(From Le Corbusier 1965, p. 80)

select days and times. Le Corbusier also designed an elaborate mechanism that would allow the removal of the roof on special occasions to let in the sun. (22#119#2903, 22#124#2914) This move converted the skylights' simple function of admitting light into an elaborate formal construction with special symbolic significance.

In the final version, Le Corbusier again redesigned the Assembly chamber and the entrance portal. First, he dropped the idea to make the roof of the paraboloid removable and instead decided to make the solar symbolism explicit by making small sculptures on the roof that in fact look like the sun and other cosmic objects.[38] Later, he replaced these with forms derived from an eighteenth-century observatory in Delhi, the Janter Manter. This observatory has huge sundials made from right-angled triangular slabs flanked by two curved blades. They are oriented north-south and the hypotenuse of the triangle is parallel to the earth's axis. The position of the shadow of the triangle on the curved blades gives the time. On the Assembly, the roof of the paraboloid—cut to form a plane parallel to the earth's axis and oriented north-south—replaces the hypotenuse of the triangle. The curving blades—much more straightened out than the ones of the observatory—are put on top of the roof. These are accompanied

Fig. 4.17. Elevation of the Assembly with "gravitational" lines of the hyperbolic paraboloid drawn in. (Drawing adapted by Leah Martin)

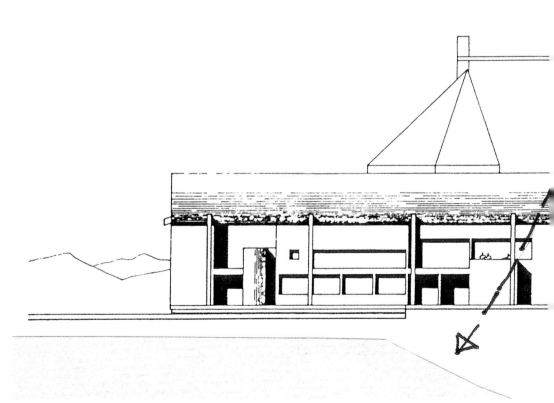

Fig. 4.18. View of the Assembly from the side, shaped like a bull. (Photograph by Norman Johnston)

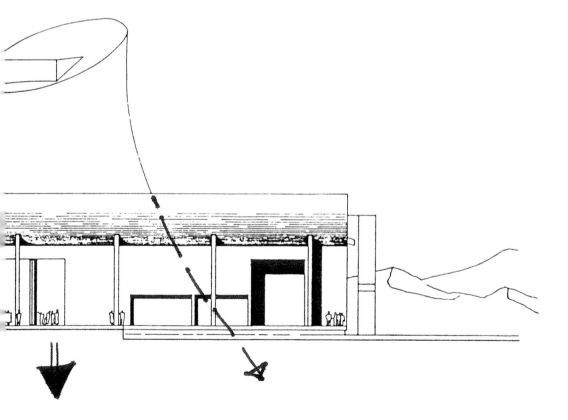

by three other parabolic shapes that signify the movement of the sun through the sky (plate 11).

The net effect of all these transformations was that the Assembly, echoing the *Taureaux* discovery, no longer remained a horizontal building but became vertical in composition. Like a typical domed construction, the Assembly's hyperbolic paraboloid is the highest point of the building, located directly over the most important space, and the crown of the main elevation of the building. Unlike the carefully masked horizontal symmetries of the High Court, the downward thrust of the hyperbolic paraboloid is naked and emphatic. The outline of its form, and the weight it carries down, can be perceptually followed through the entire building, even when it is not literally transparent. If the High Court revels in mask and play, the new Assembly, the now estranged twin, is honest and transparent in its aesthetic syntax (fig. 4.17).

The new Assembly, as a consequence, also *lost* the uncanny aesthetic of the High Court, even though it was born of an uncanny aesthetic event. Its reflections in the water pools below are just that—mere reflections. The lack of an external frame and the projecting mass of the paraboloid (along with the pyramid of the smaller assembly chamber) establish a vertical axis that is unquestionable and very stable (plate 12).

In this way, the *Taureaux* discovery set into motion an aesthetic journey whose goal was what Le Corbusier called the "re-discovery of the vertical axis." In chapter 3, we have seen how the vertical axis, filtered through biblical yearnings crossbred with a solar cosmogony, was etched into the Capitol plain as the reinscription or the restitution of the garden of Eden. Here we are witness to the particular manner in which this search was inscribed into the architectural figuration of the Assembly, and ultimately the Capitol. Aesthetic processes, like dreamwork, function through displacement and condensation; one idea may be represented by another, and an array of propositions might be distilled into a single complex construct.[39] I would suggest, therefore, that having been empowered by the *Taureaux* discovery, born of the uncanny transformation of the horizontal into the vertical, Le Corbusier *literally* memorialized that transformative event in the Assembly by the latter's transformation from a horizontal building into one that was vertical. The accompanying fetishization of the solar symbolism is probably nothing more than an opportunity that Le Corbusier seized in order to embellish the new composition, since it is about this time that he also refers to the work of Edouard Schuré, noting that the sons of Krishna were the sons of the sun.

In final form the Assembly further took on the form of the bull in the transformation of the portico from an upward-turned parasol roof, similar to that of the High Court and the Governor's Palace, into the free-form structure of a drooping U. One could, of course, argue that the U of the portico was just a minor transformation of the parasol roof form. That would not be untrue. However, the two are of fundamentally different families. The upward turned parasol roof of the Governor's Palace, with the *section* of the High Court, is fundamentally the *inverse* of the pitched roof—one of the formal types that Le Corbusier had been championing since the mid–1920s. That roof

Fig. 4.19. Le Corbusier sketch of a bull standing on the Capitol plain.
(From Le Corbusier 1953, p. 116)

belongs to the Rousseauesque idealized "house of man," which is suspended above and hovers over the ground plane.[40]

The curve of the Assembly, however, is distinctly that of a bull's horns that very fully and forcefully rests on its supports. It does not float; it does not attempt to fly. Its downward thrust is complete, like an animal standing firm on the ground (plate 13).

Indeed, if one looks at the Assembly in peripheral vision, its entire side profile looks like a giant abstracted bull, complete with horns and a hump on its back, standing waiting on the plains of Punjab. If one distorted the scale, from a distance it might even be difficult to distinguish between the sketch of a bull and that of the Assembly silhouetted against the Himalayan horizon (figs. 4.18, 4.19).

Once the "bull" Assembly was established and accepted, Le Corbusier did not return to the older orders. The horizontal Assembly, it must be remembered, belonged to the period when the Capitol aspired to be the appropriate and visible head of the city. At that time, the Governor's Palace at the northern end of the Capitol was the focal center of the composition. The *Taureaux* discovery was made after Le Corbusier's aspirations for the city had been turned down by the "betrayal" of Jeanneret and Fry in favor of the interests of the bureaucrats. (3#882) After 1952, the Assembly with its dominating paraboloid became the center of the Capitol, as assertive as the High Court was subtle (plate 14). This is, I am sure, the reason why Le Corbusier designed the Museum of Knowledge that was to replace the Governor's Palace as an ordinary box, of no special visual significance—it had to be understated so that it did not compete with the new dominance of the Assembly, which gathered the Capitol all around it. It would therefore be a mistake to go back and construct the Governor's Palace in its place now.

The Assembly and the High Court face each other across the giant Esplanade, battling each other for the viewer's attention. The distance between them is too great to make them work in concert, yet they are not sufficiently far apart to be autonomous. The Assembly is always more arresting, with its dominating paraboloid roof, much like a high-domed church, firm in its presence. On the other side of the Esplanade, the High Court draws one in, intriguing one to unravel the mysteries of its simple form, reminiscent of the Egyptian pyramids. In between them, if you stand at about the same spot where Le Corbusier drew them into his sketchbook—"sur place = exact"—you may find yourself torn, unsure of your affections.

Born of the same aesthetic core, the High Court and the Assembly are estranged twins. While the High Court is true to the original compositional kernel, the Assembly evolved, acquiring its own identity and, in the process, gathering the Capitol around itself, moving to the center of the stage. It does not even refer to the Himalayan silhouette anymore, against which Le Corbusier measured it originally.

It seems to me that the lines on the Capitol plan, the geometric squares, were like the markings of a chess board—they were regulative lines that defined the framework of engagement. The playing of the game, the artifice, was the question of sensation, of experiencing—of determining locations, dimensions, forms, and the play of shadows and reflection—and could only be done in person. These parameters were transformed and changed, constantly redefining their relationship to each other and to the land, sun, air, and water around them. And they would certainly have changed further still if more time had allowed it.

While Le Corbusier, no doubt, played this game entirely in his own mind, its objective, one might surmise, was to win the affection of those living on the Capitol Esplanade, the villagers of Kansal. Having so romanticized the noble savage, and being so convinced of the fundamental communicability of the aesthetic composition, Le Corbusier must have shuddered at the thought of the very real possibility—and one that was impossible to verify one way or the other—that the villagers of Kansal might not understand his buildings. Today, this is still impossible to ascertain for this author, just as it is impossible for me to verify whether Le Corbusier ever meant all that I have understood his buildings to be. Nonetheless, it would be disingenuous to deny that one always writes, and designs, with the hope of verification.

# Architectural Symbolism and the Vagaries of Political Claims

By the time the Open Hand was finally constructed and raised in the Capitol it was 1985, almost thirty years after Le Corbusier had proposed it. Chandigarh was under siege then, ravaged by autonomy-seeking Sikh terrorists, who were killing random people on state transport buses almost every day and at will. Under the circumstances, wrote Rajneesh Wattas, a professor in the local school of architecture, the making of the Open Hand was meaningless, because it was the symbol of an ideology that did not respond to the real needs of the people and was incomprehensible to them. "Undoubtedly," Wattas argued, monuments have their architectural use in acting as "symbols of passion that make people love their cities and countries, but as the time gap between their original conception and the actual realization widens, they stand in danger of losing their spiritual quintessence."[1]

A young student in the college of architecture then, I immediately dashed off a response letter to the journal where Wattas's article was printed. On the contrary, I argued, the Open Hand symbolized the now even greater necessity of exchanging with an open mind, "open to receive, open to give." "In our time of uncertain peace, when narrow and parochial interest and close-fisted policies seem to dominate the scene, a symbol like the Open Hand, far from losing its 'spiritual quintessence,' assumes desperate importance," I wrote.[2]

But yet, the belated construction of the Hand forced one to wonder how it was that we had arrived at a situation where we were so besieged, enclosed by sandbagged paramilitary forces, so distant from the free and open ideals that were represented by the monument. They were intended to be common currency once, the aspirations of a new nation; and why was the Hand not built then, in its time, when it would have been in its prime?

Wattas was, however, right about one thing—it did not matter what the Open Hand stood for. The question was: how was it understood? The chief administrator of the city (or, who knows, it might have been the publicity manager) decided to aggressively adopt the Hand as the symbol and sign of the city early in the 1980s. The Open Hand made for a convincing graphic, and regardless of its intended symbolic content, the Chandigarh Administration set about printing and embossing it on every piece of stationary and official document. They even constructed two more Hands at the border posts where the highway enters Chandigarh territory (fig. 5.1). Many of the city's commercial establishments integrated it into their own graphics. I even found a Hand on my driving license (fig. 5.2). And the tourist brochure for the city advertised the Hand as a symbol of "Indian civilization's greedlessness and magnanimity." The Hand is everywhere in Chandigarh today.

Under the circumstances I was chagrined and somewhat surprised on my first trip to Paris, to find that the Fondation Le Corbusier had adopted "our" Open Hand as its sign, too. It is on everything that emerges from the Fondation, as it is on the cover of each one of the thirty volumes of the *Le Corbusier Archives*. How could Chandigarh's Open Hand, *our* Open Hand, also be their Open Hand? Of course, I soon I realized that the Fondation's Open Hand was really a different Open Hand from Chandigarh's Open Hand. For both institutions it was just an icon—a graphic that signified very different things, connected only by circumstantial events of history.

What is the "spiritual quintessence" of an architectural symbol? Of any work of art? For the Fondation it signified the person, life, and ideology of Le Corbusier, and for the administration it symbolized the city, its legacy, and its aspirations. As a citizen of Chandigarh, I was disputing the Fondation's right to an icon. And both our claims, intent on exploiting the iconic value of the Hand, were basically independent of the actual history and circumstances under which Le Corbusier had proposed it, and that had forced Jawaharlal Nehru to refuse to have it built, back in the late 1950s.

Fig. 5.1 The "other" Open Hand at the entrance to Chandigarh. (Photograph by Navneet Saxena)

Fig. 5.2 Chandigarh's official driver's license with a stamp of the Open Hand.

On 8 May 1958, Le Corbusier wrote Jawaharlal Nehru a letter beseeching him to sanction the money necessary to have the Open Hand constructed in Chandigarh. Le Corbusier had been writing to Nehru since the mid-1950s to have the Hand built, but finally in June 1958 Nehru wrote back decisively:

> As for your proposal of "The Open Hand" to be put up as a symbol, just at present we are in such a difficult financial position that we have stopped any kind of work that is not considered inescapable. I can very well understand your enthusiasm and your disappointment at any delay in realizing your conception. But, there are so many matters pressing in upon us that we are compelled to delay many things that we might otherwise do.[3]

The fledgling new Indian state was never flush with funds. The making of Chandigarh was a gesture that was considered to be of extraordinary significance and accordingly was financed through extraordinary means. It would not have been possible without Nehru's personal interest and financial assistance from the central government. Under the circumstances, Le Corbusier's request to Nehru was arguably neither inappropriate nor extravagant.

Even so, Nehru obviously felt constrained to reject Le Corbusier's request, "because there are so many matters pressing upon us." Why was the Open Hand so important for Le Corbusier? And why did Nehru feel constrained to refuse the funds for it? And finally, how did the Open Hand get built? Architecture is a crossroad for life's forces; we enact our life-worlds on its stage set. More life stories live through a work of architecture than can ever be accounted for in a single narrative. In this chapter, I narrate the story of the Open Hand from multiple perspectives, which belong to different life-worlds that, in a sense, only happen to be united by the fact that they refer to the same sculptural object. Yet, I would argue, all these worlds have equivalent rights to the graphing of the Hand's history. I will end with a discussion of still other Hands, vying for attention, asserting other claims (plate 15).

## First Open Hand: Le Corbusier's Open Hand

A handprint, the first signature, is one of the oldest recordings of having "been there." It conveys identity through a strong visceral presence. A very clean imprint of Le Corbusier's own hand can be found on a 1950s fresco, "L'Étoile de Mer," at Cap Martin[4] (fig. 5.3). One can also recall that Le Corbusier repeatedly emphasized that he had painted the Enamel Door of the

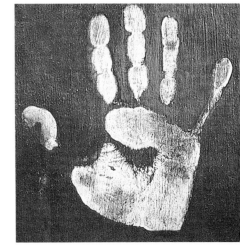

Fig. 5.3. Le Corbusier's handprint on "L'Étoile de Mer." (From Le Corbusier 1970, p. 189)

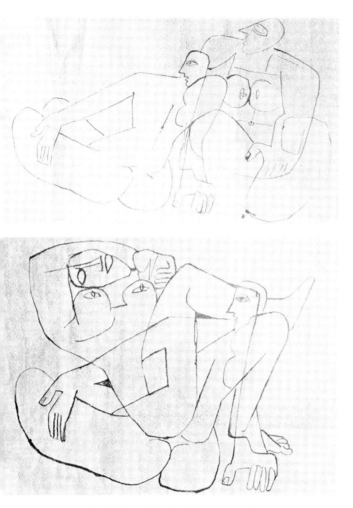

Fig. 5.4. Le Corbusier's Algerian studies for a monumental mural.
(Reproduced in von Moos 1985, p. 319)

209. Le Corbusier, *The red hand*, oil on canvas, 1930. Collection Heidi Weber, Zurich (photo courtesy of Heidi Weber, Zurich)

210. Egyptian hieroglyph for the divine RA (from S. Giedion, *The Eternal Pres-*

Fig. 5.5. Le Corbusier's "The Red Hand."
(Reproduced in von Moos 1985, p. 320)

Assembly "with his own hands," and that he concluded his short presentation at the dedication of the Door with a similar haptic message, exhorting his audience to remember that he was "an engraver of watches; to-day, only the dimension has changed."[5]

One could easily be led to believe that Le Corbusier's Open Hand, being from his own hand and of his own hand, was meant to be imbued with presence and was, as such, something of a graphic signature. This would lead us to Mary Sekler's reading that the Hand betrays Le Corbusier's roots in the Arts and Crafts Movement and his faith in the moral superiority of the work done by the body over that of the mind.[6]

The Hand, however, is not preponderant in Le Corbusier's work as an imprinted signifier of presence. Rather, it is used as a stylized and abstracted symbolic form in his

Fig. 5.6. Le Corbusier's mural "Graffite à Cap Martin." (Reproduced in von Moos 1985, p. 321)

paintings. It occurs sometimes alone and at other times is conjoined with another hand. It can be identified first in Le Corbusier's 1928 painting entitled "Handlike Gloves." Two paintings of the early 1930s, "Hand and Flint," and "The Red Hand," are very similar compositionally. Both show the hand, a left hand, extending a greeting outward. As Le Corbusier became more intrigued by the female figure, the primary subject matter for his later paintings, the hand, as well as its relationship to the female body, became increasingly abstract and symbolic. In 1949, for instance, Le Corbusier decorated the walls of the lounge of the Swiss Pavilion (a dormitory for Swiss students at the Cité Universitaire in Paris) with a winged female creature, based on a poem by Mallarmé, a creature whose open wing is supported and nestled in a large open hand that is also a gesture of a caress (figs. 5.4–5.6).

In these paintings, the hand is usually in the foreground, occupying a prominent part of the composition. More than just the symbolic culmination of the expressive turn of the body, it is a strong and forceful gesture, detached from the body, an entity unto itself. It indicates direction and a sense of impending action. It is the instrument of work.

This sense of agency is also prominent in some photographs published by Le Corbusier. The famous one illustrating the modular construction of the Unités, for instance, has a hand (presumably Le Corbusier's own) "plugging" one the apartments into the structural grid. Here the hand suggests not only the simplicity of modular

Fig. 5.7. The hand as an expression of agency, inserting dwelling units into a model of the *Unité*. (Reproduced in von Moos 1985, p. 110)

construction, but also the agency, man's protean creativity, that realizes it[7] (fig. 5.7).

Other photographs published by Le Corbusier posit the hand as the signature of power. In one of them, Le Corbusier has Nehru at his side pointing at something with the plan of Chandigarh in his hand. In the foreground, relatively exaggerated by perspective, Nehru's hand stands for the executive authority and the invocation to action that enabled Chandigarh to be[8] (fig. 5.8). This photograph is an echo of a drawing Le Corbusier included in his *Œuvre* of Louis XIV issuing the commandment to build Versailles, which shows the king gesturing with his hand at the plan to indicate his intention[9] (fig. 5.9). In all these depictions, the hand enables things to be; it is the hand of power issuing commandments.

The hand as a sign of the ontological genesis of moral work, the

Fig. 5.8. Nehru's hand as an agent of power. (From Le Corbusier 1953, p. 152)

Fig. 5.9. Louis XIV's hand as an agent of power. (Reproduced in Krustrup 1991, p. 108)

Fig. 5.10. The hand in the Monument in Memory of Vaillant-Couturier. (From Le Corbusier 1946, p. 10)

form in which it is celebrated by a Ruskinian ideology, is very different from the hand as the authoritative symbol of work, the meaning it acquires in most of Le Corbusier's paintings. While the former mythologizes the autonomous agency of handwork, the latter is a political metaphor abstracting the instrumental nature of the hand as the origin of action. It is the latter that will take us to Chandigarh, even if embroiled in a cesspool of politics.

The direct prototype for Chandigarh's Open Hand is the Monument in Memory of Valliant-Couturier that Le Corbusier designed in 1938 for the left-wing mayor of Villejuif in France. Composed of an open book, a huge bust with a screaming mouth, and an open gesturing hand of comradeship, all of which is supported by an enormous vertical slab, this monument was the closest Le Corbusier came to socialist realism. If the book stands for knowledge, and the open mouth for voice and protest, it is the hand, like the communist hammer and sickle, that signifies the agent of work and transformation in this unbuilt socialist monument (fig. 5.10).

Le Corbusier himself, however, repeatedly insisted that the Open Hand was not a political creation, but that of an architect:

> The Open Hand Monument … is not a political emblem, not the creation of a politician. It is an architect's creation, it is the fruit of architecture. This creation is a specific case of human neutrality; he who creates something does so by virtue of the laws of physics, chemistry, biology, ethics, aesthetics, all bound in a single shelf; a house, a city. This is different from politics in that the architect's equation requires physics, chemistry, the strength of materials, the law of gravity, biology—without which everything cracks, everything breaks, everything collapses. It is like the airplane; either it flies or it doesn't, and the verdict is delivered quickly.[10]

This quotation suggests that architecture, as well as the Hand, was solely the work of "human neutrality" for Le Corbusier, a product of, and only answerable to, fundamental physical laws. But as we have seen, the hand (and Le Corbusier's architecture in general) is answerable to much more than physical laws. If one searches elsewhere in his writings, one finds that Le Corbusier in fact names the Hand as his only *political* creation. In a letter to his friend Claude Petit in September 1964, Le Corbusier wrote:

> I never did politics (all the while respecting those who did—the good ones); but I made one political gesture, that of the Open Hand. The day that one of the two parties dividing the world in the interest of two different natures made me choose sides, as a moral duty. On the plane to Bogota, at that moment in 1951, I drew "The Open Hand."[11]

I would therefore suggest that, his assertions to the contrary notwithstanding, the Hand is not as much about what architecture is or is not, as it is about what for Le Corbusier everyday politics generally *is*, i.e., that it is *not* answerable to any laws, that its verdicts are always open to contestation, while one always has to wait for its answers. Le Corbusier never ceased to complain vocally and bitterly about the vagaries and exigencies of politics that had prevented him from realizing his visions: the League of Nations, the Palace of the Soviets, the United Nations building, and even Chandigarh. "A great number of really good projects, let's be modest enough to admit it," he bitterly wrote in his *Final Testament*, "were torpedoed by the bureaucrats."[12] In this sense, the Open Hand was Le Corbusier's apolitical answer to the world of politics, embodying his conception of what political ideals should really be.

Le Corbusier designed the seventy-six-foot-high Hand made of burnished steel to be mounted on a central shaft with ball bearings that allow it to rotate in response to wind pressure. He designed it to do that, Le Corbusier wrote tersely, "not to show the incertitude of ideas, but to indicate symbolically the direction of the wind."[13] While "the uncertainty of ideas" is recognizably a negative reference to the vagaries of political ethics, Le Corbusier's characterization of the function of the Open Hand as that of merely turning in the wind gives one pause to think. Is it meant to function like a flag? The symbolism of this function is either too obvious (a weather vane) and commonplace, or is veiled and metaphoric.

The reference to the "direction of the wind," I would suggest, is parodic. While the direction of the wind does change as frequently and as whimsically as political ideas (and that is the parody), the symbolism, I think, refers to the constancy of the Hand that can maintain its position, firmly upheld on its vertical shaft, swiveling to accommodate— like grass—the changing wind, while maintaining its fundamental character. This is how Le Corbusier characterized his own political idealism.

At another place, Le Corbusier described the conception of the Open Hand as a "spontaneous event," probably on the flight to Bogota. It was born, he describes, as

> a sort of a cockle floating above the horizon, but the stretched fingers showed the open hand like a vast shell. Later … the idea returned taking a different form. It was no longer a shell but a fan, a silhouette. It is the value of the silhouette which developed through the years. Little by little the open hand appeared as a possibility in great architectural compositions.[14]

The drawings that Le Corbusier is referring to can be found in the second of the two *Nivola Albums* that he was drawing in the early 1950s.[15] A sequence of sketches, starting 17 February 1950, chronicle a story symbolic of birthing. In the earliest sketches the hand looks something like a baseball mitt, underscored by a horizon line. These are followed by sketches of naked women with their hands exaggerated and emphasized in the action of a caress and salutation. And then finally there is the birth of the new Open Hand, distinctly floating above a horizon line, with five naked women in the foreground, devoted witnesses to this birth. One lying and four sitting—the composite image of the women, one notes, forms a hand in itself. These two hands, with the horizon line in between, are encircled and then repeated on the next page. And then finally, the Hand floats by itself, without witnesses, in a sketch entitled "version B" (fig. 5.11, plate 16).

Fig. 5.11. Genesis of the Hand. (From Le Corbusier [c. 1950–1960], pp. 5, 11, 17, 19, 25. See also plate 1.)

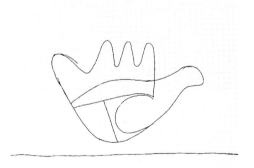

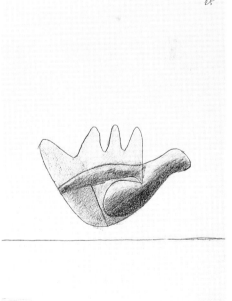

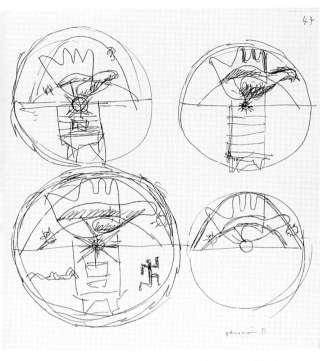

**Fig. 5.12** Sketch for Le Corbusier medal. (From Le Corbusier [c.1950–60], p. 47)

Later in the same *Nivola Album*, there is a sketch that Le Corbusier made for the medal with which he was honored on the completion of the Unité d'Habitation at Marseilles in 1951. This medal has Le Corbusier's bust on one side and the Open Hand on the other. The Hand is drawn into a composition that approximates that of the painting on the outside of the Assembly's Enamel Door. With a section of Marseilles Unité below the horizon line, the Open Hand is drawn into the sky with the catenary curves of the summer and winter suns (fig. 5.12).

The Assembly's Enamel Door was painted after this medal was designed, and their distinctive formal similarity evidences that they are developments of the same idea. The logics of formal composition help discover parallels between the Door and the Hand. An overlay of the two, justified along the horizon line would show that the outline of the Hand is roughly equivalent to that of the yellow curve in the middle of the upper section of the painting on the Door. This suggests that the yellow curve in the enamel door is the abstracted representation of the Open Hand.

If this is the case, it also suggests that the Open Hand does not belong to the terrestrial world below, but to the world of the sky, the heavens above. Le Corbusier undertook innumerable further studies of "version B," and in all of these the Hand hovers above the horizon line as if it were an abstract drawing inked into the sky. A two-dimensional form that never really straddles the three dimensions of space, the Hand, in other words, is never grounded; it always points upwards and gathers the sky in its catenary curves. It floats in space as if painted on the sky; and if one indeed peers at it in the distance, one can imagine it to be a tracing of a mythical constellation in the sky, a divine sign signifying perhaps the astrological dawn of a new era.

In official documents, Le Corbusier named the Open Hand the symbol of the ethics of the Second Machine Age: "open to receive, open to give." The problem, according to him was that the world followed a closefisted policy, instead of holding forth an open hand that would be "open to receive and open to give," which for him was "the ineluctable destiny of the mechanical civilization, which today, making use of its machines in a dangerous way, forgets that its open hand shall be filled with consumer goods."[16] Here the Open Hand is the symbol of an era of prosperity brought about by the equitable distribution of machine-made goods—a quasi-socialist idea, directed against the economics of capitalism, masked in idealist garb.

By the end of his life, Le Corbusier had invested the Hand with even greater expectations. For him it was the final act that would establish something of a new religion, with him as its new messiah. In the *Final Testament* he wrote of it as a statement of personal accomplishment, "a stage of life" identified with the completion of Chandigarh:

> Before joining the stars (some day), I shall be happy to see, in Chandigarh, in front of the Himalaya soaring up on the horizon, this Open Hand, which marks for Père Corbu an accomplished fact, a stage of life. I beseech you, André Malraux, you, my associates, you, my friends, to help me realize this sign of the Open Hand in the skies of Chandigarh, city desired by Nehru, the disciple of Gandhi.[17]

A continued archeology of the Hand might lead us into a symptomatology of unrequited desires and personal preoccupations of the kind associated with the painting on the Enamel Door, about which I wrote in chapter 3. At this point, however, I would like to focus on one particular event connected with the Hand that will help take us into the world of the Nehruvian state, the purported client of Chandigarh's Open Hand.

## Second Open Hand: The Politics of Non-Alignment and Secularism

On 22 July 1955, Le Corbusier wrote Nehru a letter making the case for the construction of the Hand as a political symbol. He argued it in terms of an appropriate response to the dilemma of the Cold War. Le Corbusier stated that on 17 April 1949, at the World Congress of the Upholders of Peace:

> they laid a frightful pressure on me. They tried to use and misuse my name and practiced the threat of the bullet in the nape of the neck. I replied with a written declaration to the World Congress. …
>
> "They wish to place us on the horns of a USA—USSR dilemma. This is the result of a lack of information. … I refuse to play into your hands and accept the conditions of the dilemma which may be terrible."[18]

This refusal on his part, Le Corbusier continued, led him to the Open Hand:

> I was possessed by the tragic quandary which was offered here and there under the outrageous term of "TO COMMIT ONESELF." I picked up a drawing of 1948 representing an open hand above the sky-line; five women grouped on the ground see it rise to view. From then onwards I only kept the hand in my drawing its outline getting more and more pure. I drew it during my travels. It took shape.[19]

"It took shape." Refusing to commit himself, maintaining independence in the face of an abominable choice, in this letter Le Corbusier projects the Hand as a symbol of this ideal. He proposes it, in other words, as a symbol of political non-alignment.

Although he characterizes it as his own private commitment, Le Corbusier no doubt was eminently aware that non-alignment was the centerpiece of Nehru's foreign policy. While "the modern world is torn between the USA and the URSS [*sic*]," Le Corbusier reminded Nehru, the "Asiatic East is gathering together." "This monument," Le Corbusier invoked in conclusion to his letter, "will have far-reaching ethical consequences. I am sure that by dressing in this place 'The Open Hand,' India will make a gesture which will corroborate your intervention which is so decisive at the crucial moment of the machinist evolution and its threats."[20]

History reveals that the "intervention" that Le Corbusier was offering to corroborate was the landmark Afro-Asian conference (Bandung 1955) that led to the formation of the Non-Aligned Movement. In his letter to Nehru, Le Corbusier was drawing a connection between the Open Hand and NAM on the basis of a shared ideology. Nehru's speech to the Bandung Conference Political Committee set the agenda for NAM and was widely reported in the international press. It is worth quoting extensively here, to understand Nehru, and to see if Le Corbusier's offer to "corroborate" can itself be corroborated.

Nehru opened his speech by indicting the supposed wisdom of the "great nations":

> We have just had the advantage of listening to the distinguished leader of the Turkish Delegation who … gave us an able statement of what I might call one side representing the views of one of the major blocs existing at the present time in the world. I have no doubt that an equally able disposition could be made on the part of the other bloc. I belong to neither and I propose to belong to neither whatever happens in the world. If we have to stand alone, we will stand by ourselves, whatever happens … and we propose to face all consequences. … We do not agree with the communist teachings, we do not agree with the anticommunist teachings, because they are both based on wrong principles. …
>
> I speak with the greatest respect of these Great Powers because they are not only great in military might but in development, in culture, in civilization. But I do submit that greatness sometimes brings quite false values, false standards. When they begin to think in terms of military strength—whether it be the United Kingdom, the Soviet Union or the U.S.A.—then they are going away from the right track and the result of that will be that the overwhelming might of one country will conquer the world. Thus far the world has succeeded in preventing that; I cannot speak for the future.

Even a cursory reading evidences that Nehru's words are faithfully echoed in Le Corbusier's letter. The former's choice to "stand by ourselves, whatever happens," for instance, is the latter's "refusal to play"; Nehru's accusation of the great nations to be "preparing false standards" is what Le Corbusier characterized as the misguided work of the "First Machine Age." Continuing, describing the consequences of war, Nehru painted a picture of the Apocalypse:

> You cannot stop these things. … Annihilation will result not only in the countries engaged in war, but owing to the radioactive waves which go thousands and thousands of miles it will destroy everything. That is the position. It is not an academic position; it is not a position of discussing ideologies; nor is it a position of discussing past history. It is looking at the world as it is today.

Again, Nehru's defense of his position as "not a position of discussing ideologies [but as] looking at the world as it is today," is not that different from the effort to steer clear of the "incertitude of political ideas," as Le Corbusier had put it. And, finally, the only answer for Nehru was a critical independence that assures a measure of dignity—the refusal, in Le Corbusier's words, "to play into your hands and accept the conditions of the dilemma which may be terrible":

> So far as I am concerned, it does not matter what war takes place; we will not take part in it unless we have to defend ourselves. If I join any of these big groups I lose my identity. … If all the world were to be divided up between these two big blocs what would be the result? The inevitable result would be war. Therefore every step that takes place in reducing that area in the world which may be called the unaligned area is a dangerous step and leads to war. It reduces that objective, that balance, that outlook which other countries without military might can perhaps exercise.
> Has it come to this, that the leaders of thought who have given religions and all kinds of things to the world have to tag on to this kind of group or that and be hangers-on of this party or the other, carrying out their wishes and occasionally giving an idea? It is most degrading and humiliating to any self-respecting people or nation. It is an intolerable thought to me that the great countries of Asia and Africa should come out of bondage into freedom only to degrade themselves or humiliate themselves in this way.[21]

Nehru's speech was delivered in April 1955 and Le Corbusier wrote his letter, professing that the ideals of the Open Hand were those of the Non-Aligned Movement, in July 1955, barely three months later. Based on Le Corbusier's letter and Nehru's speech there would seem to be an extraordinary synergy between the two men, and there is the distinct possibility that they did, in fact, share their ideals. Their personalities certainly did match in many ways. Both of them prided themselves on being independent thinkers, committed to the belief that a well-reasoned and articulated perspective would find its own resonance, justification, and eventual vindication. Nehru, like Le Corbusier, was a committed enlightenment modernist and was a true believer in the idea that science and technology could be deployed in a socialized manner to engender an alternative, liberated society. He detested the wreckages of history and convention, and actively encouraged new thinking. Both of them established a significant reputation for articulating a visionary third alternative, and, as history would have it, both of them by the end of their lives felt that their achievement had been severely compromised by the politics of greed.

The commonplace view is that Nehru was a great supporter of Le Corbusier and often took issue on his behalf. There are letters in the files from Nehru to the chief minister of Punjab, intervening on Le Corbusier's behalf to have one administrative official removed (K. S. Narang) and another reinstated (P. L. Verma). He spoke out against his own Public Works Department after being prodded by Le Corbusier, and suggested that the department consider the latter's unconventional housing proposals because they were supposedly "more in terms of Indian conditions."[22] He even publicly defended Le Corbusier at a meeting of the Indian Institute of Engineers, albeit in a somewhat backhanded way:

> Now I have welcomed very greatly, one experiment … Chandigarh. Many people argue about it, some like it, some dislike it. It is totally immaterial whether you like it or not. It is the biggest thing in India of this kind. That is why I welcome it. It is the biggest thing because it hits you on the head and makes you think. You may squirm at the impact but it makes you think and imbibe new ideas, and the one thing that India requires in so many fields is to be hit on the head so that you may think.[23]

The exceptional cooperation between Le Corbusier's conception of the Second Machine Age, and Nehru's ideals of the Non-Aligned Movement as the coming-together of the third world countries, makes it much more difficult to understand why Nehru nevertheless felt compelled to refuse funding for the Hand. Le Corbusier has been accused of pandering to authority whenever he felt it served his interests, while maintaining a public persona of absolute disdain for worldly honors. As the timing of Le Corbusier's letter indicates, there may certainly be some truth to that in the case of the Hand. The Open Hand was a personal obsession of Le Corbusier's and he may simply have been trying to find a way to make Nehru think that its symbolism and aspirations were the same as those of the Non-Aligned Movement. This accusation would be supported by the fact that Le Corbusier never publicly announced that the Open Hand was connected to non-alignment, just as he did not declare himself a part of that movement.[24] Nehru may have realized this and therefore may have simply chosen to avoid the issue.

Yet, even if Nehru felt that Le Corbusier might be opportunistic, it could have served Nehru's interests to pick up on the Open Hand and to integrate it into his own agenda. Nehru remained a vocal and active advocate of the NAM until his death in 1964, so there is no reason to think that he might have rethought his commitment to its ideals, and Le Corbusier implored the world to build the Hand until his last days as well.

Why then? To understand the circumstances surrounding Nehru's refusal to sanction funding for the Hand, we have to examine, not the politics on the international stage, but those on the domestic soil of Punjab, of which Chandigarh was the new symbolically charged capital. We have to, in other words, see the situation from Nehru's micropolitical perspective.

### Third Open Hand: The Micropolitics of the Nehruvian Nation-State

Chandigarh's Open Hand has a lesser-known twin—one proposed atop Bhakra Nangal, a massive hydroelectric dam, about one hundred miles north from Chandigarh. Early in the 1950s, Nehru asked Le Corbusier to propose an aesthetic plan for Bhakra.[25] Nehru's intention no doubt was to get suggestions for ways of integrating the massive constructions of the dam with its surrounding landscape. When Le Corbusier visited the site, he chose not to give undue importance to other architectural features, as the "dam itself [was] a very powerful structure." Instead, Le Corbusier proposed to create rudimentary additions like a walkway for visitors. And, along with that, he proposed that another Open Hand be constructed at a vantage point atop the dam as a crowning feature[26] (fig. 5.13).

Nehru's invitation to Le Corbusier to work on the Bhakra Dam was not simply intended to expand the latter's responsibilities to an unrelated project. Chandigarh and Bhakra, in fact, were closely connected. Not only were they two of the most prominent state-sponsored projects of Punjab, but both also embodied Nehruvian hopes of modernity. Like Chandigarh, Bhakra was also intended to deliver and symbolize the future. Nehru called Bhakra one of the "temples of modern India," a claim that while it

Fig. 5.13. Drawing of the Open Hand atop the Bhakra dam.

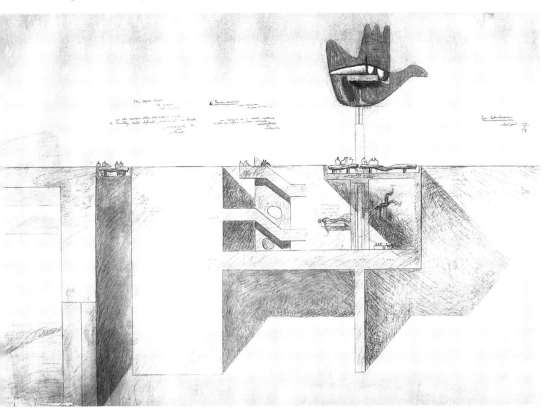

was rhetorical was also, quite literally, not far from the professed ideologies of the Nehruvian state. By constitution, the modern Nehruvian nation-state strictly adopted the Western division of church and state. It followed the Enlightenment model of the secular nation-state that was independent from and yet guaranteed the freedom of all religious identities. By aspiration, however, modernity was something of a new religion. Even if he never directly posited it, there can be no doubt that Nehru hoped that the ideals of progress and prosperity that could potentially be unleashed by larger-than-life projects such as Bhakra would help overcome and render obsolete the partisan factions of religious and ethnic identities, of which he had always been wary, and which had resulted in a violent partition, confirming his worst suspicions. Bhakra, like Chandigarh, was freighted with great expectations—even if it was not meant to be the literal symbol of a new religion, it was certainly proffered as a catalyst for the obsolescence of older ones.

Modernity, in the Nehruvian syntax, was not only unfettered by the past, but also an instrument *to* unfetter the past. As I have argued in chapter 2, in the Nehruvian world the "new" and the "good" were interchangeable. By the same logic that Chandigarh's modernity was to be delivered by making it "unfettered by the traditions of the past," the Tennessee Valley Authority–inspired hydroelectric dams were intended to become the new "temples of modern India." Nehru, indeed, was a prophet of a new quasi-religion, with Bhakra and Chandigarh being two of the prominent symbols of its new faith.

Such were the affects of Bhakra. The actual effects of Bhakra, however, were quite different.[27]

Because of its focus on a modern secular ideology, there was always the danger that the new nation-state itself, by forming a single target, could also become an instigator of sectarian forces, the very forces that it was created against. This was especially the case in Punjab, where religious violence was a living precedent in the wake of partition. There was, in other words, the very present danger that the Sikhs might claim autonomy in the same way the Muslims did.[28]

Indeed, the seeds for Punjab's further partition were already in place at Independence. The Akali Dal, an autonomous Sikh political party, had formulated its identity through its own sectarian agenda even prior to independence. After 1947, the Akali Dal began to define itself as a specifically "Sikh" party, generally opposed to Nehru's Congress Party that was at the helm in the national government. Immediately following independence, the Akali Dal voiced a demand for an autonomous "Punjabi Suba," based on the linguistic criterion, which Nehru of course vehemently opposed.

Part of the Nehruvian plan was that the technological and economic gains of Bhakra would offset and quell the sectarian claims in Punjab. Besides providing electric power, the dam's largest impact was expected to be in the agricultural economy. Punjab was already considered to be the breadbasket of India, but its traditional agricultural sector was limited to the central tracts of the state, which had abundant rainfall in the monsoons. Private wells had been necessary to irrigate the regions in the peripheries away from the rivers, which had significantly lower rainfalls and large desert areas. One of Bhakra's important objectives, therefore, was to expand the agricultural land by developing an irrigation system consisting of an extensive network of canals which carried water from the central reservoir to the outlying areas of Punjab.

However, instead of quelling the demand for an autonomous Punjabi Suba, the Bhakra canal projects further inflamed political unrest in the state on grounds of discrimination and favoritism. To begin with, although their costs were predominantly borne by the central farmers, whose land revenue assessments were higher because of their greater cropping densities and acreage, the canals primarily benefited the southern and the eastern tracts of the province. Furthermore, the drainage of the central region was seriously disrupted by the canals, whose raised banks inevitably caused flooding upstream during the rainy season. This caused widespread loss of cropland. As a compensation for the central farmers, the government aided the development of private wells which were of no benefit to either the mountainous or the southern tracts.

As a consequence a political crisis ensued, and the government of Punjab, which had a substantial majority of representatives from the regions outside the central tracts, found itself repeatedly unable to reconcile the conflicting sets of needs. The claim for an autonomous "Punjabi Suba" gained a new lease on life as political violence took to the streets. To make matters worse, there was a drought in 1965 and Punjab had to be declared a "food zone" by the national government. This meant that although the Punjabi farmers had a bumper harvest, they were restricted from moving and selling their crops outside the designated areas, which prevented them from reaching markets of high demand. While this step was intended to control inflation, it was perceived as an ethnic and religious bias and as an infringement on the rights of the rural population of the central and northern tracts of Punjab, comprised mostly of Sikh farmers.[29]

Portrayed as the flagship project of a broader series of agricultural reforms, Bhakra eventually collapsed under the weight of its own symbolism. As the Punjab's political crisis raged on, Bhakra was demonized not only for grievances related to the unequal distribution of its waters, but for all social and economic grievances associated with the Nehruvian reforms it was meant to symbolize.

Partap Singh Kairon, the chief minister of Punjab and a close friend and supporter of Nehru, was assassinated in February 1965. In the elections that followed, the Akali Dal formed the provincial government in Punjab and the Congress Party came into power in the central government, with Indira Gandhi, Nehru's daughter, as the prime minister. Indira Gandhi deemed the Nehruvian policy a failure and decided to accede to the demand for a Punjabi Suba. In 1966, the Punjabi Suba was finally created when Punjab was divided into a linguistically Punjab state and the two Hindi-speaking states of Haryana and Himachal Pradesh. (fig. 5.14)

With the creation of the Punjabi Suba, Chandigarh was transformed into a Union Territory, which meant it would be administered by the central government and not by any state government. Yet at the same time it also housed the governments of both the

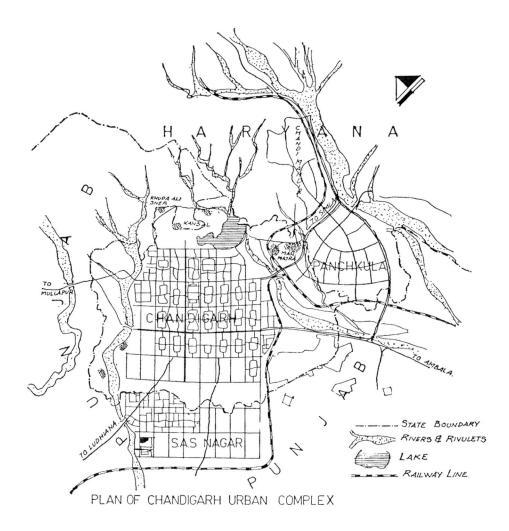

PLAN OF CHANDIGARH URBAN COMPLEX

**Fig. 5.14** Map of the greater Chandigarh urban complex. (From Prakash 1983)

states of Punjab and Haryana. The boundaries between Punjab and Haryana were drawn up in such a way that Chandigarh came to be located right on the boundary line—although in time Chandigarh was supposed to become a part of Punjab with the construction of Haryana's new capital. In the same vein, the Assembly building in the Capitol was divided to hold the two legislative assemblies, as were the offices of the Secretariat. The city's own local government, the Chandigarh Administration, was housed in a separate building in the heart of the city.

In this way, Chandigarh became a city administered autonomously by unelected officials appointed from New Delhi and played host to the two "rival" governments of Punjab and Haryana. While such a strange, compromised arrangement was no doubt practical, the arrangement can also be read as the spatialization of the historical compromise effected in the partition of Punjab along linguistic lines.

Nehru's letter to Le Corbusier, written in 1958, spoke of the "so many matters pressing in upon us that we are compelled to delay many things that we might otherwise do." In the above I have tried to trace out the broad picture that is made of these "pressing matters," the effects of which continued well beyond Nehru's lifetime. Under the circumstances, the erection of the Open Hand, I would therefore posit, was simply not apposite—it did not remain unbuilt for financial reasons and certainly not for reasons of lack of cultural translation. On the contrary, the Open Hand could not be built precisely because it would have been understood too well—as the blighted crown atop a temple that was no longer in grace.

Identity is a political matter, a claim made by association. Due to the unanticipated effects of the redistribution of water, the Bhakra Dam's reputation, along with that of Nehru's entire project of modernization, was under severe censure. With the breakdown of the Nehruvian project, its symbols were naturally in question. Chandigarh, indelibly associated with Bhakra, was fundamentally implicated in the process and was headed for partition. The city's Open Hand, identical to that of Bhakra, was caught in the fray. This would explain why the Open Hand by the mid-1960s had become a popular joke among the architects of Chandigarh—as the open hand of the traffic policeman held up to stop the flow of Bhakra's waters.[30]

## Construction: Other Open Hands

Nehru died in 1964. It took another twenty years, and a lot of political jostling, before the Open Hand was finally constructed in Chandigarh. By then the Hand meant something entirely different. The one at Bhakra was never built and was never seriously considered.

Only in December 1972 did Prime Minister Indira Gandhi finally sanction funding for Chandigarh's Open Hand.[31] It was a good year for Indira Gandhi: she was flush with victory after a war with Pakistan, which was followed by a landslide electoral victory in the country. The Congress Party that had always campaigned on the platform of modernization, came to power in Punjab as well at that time. Indira Gandhi obviously felt confident enough of her position vis-à-vis the factional politics of the state to reinstate the old symbols of her father.

Her expectations, however, were short-lived and the Akali Dal soon launched an agitation inaugurating a new series of political jousts that resulted in both the Congress Party as well as the Akali Dal losing legitimacy and power in the state. Late in the 1970s, power was literally wrested out of the state's hands by militant, orthodox Sikh groups who resorted to terrorism to have their voices heard and their demands met. In 1984 Indira Gandhi ordered a military attack on the Golden Temple in Amritsar, 175 miles from Chandigarh. This was the holiest Sikh shrine and hideout of militant leaders Sant Jarnail Singh Bhindranwale and Amrik Singh. They were killed along with hundreds of Sikhs; in October 1984, Indira Gandhi was assassinated by her Sikh bodyguards in retribution.

In the midst of these tribulations, thanks to the little window of opportunity that

Fig. 5.15. The hand as the Congress Party's election symbol.

opened up in 1972, the Open Hand did receive official funding, and was finally put in place in 1985. It is, I think, only a coincidence that Rajiv Gandhi, Indira Gandhi's son, was in power then, once again supported by a massive national mandate.

By 1985 Nehruvian politics was a thing of the past, and the Hand simply was an old relic, disassociated from its history. Since then the administration of the city has aggressively propagated the Hand as the visible symbol of Chandigarh. The Hand does make a memorable silhouette and prints well on official stationary. The Administration, it is quite possible, may have simply been inspired by the graphic possibilities of the Hand and may have acted to adopt it oblivious of the original symbolism and the subsequent trials in its history. They have certainly been successful. Today the Hand is remembered and recognized only as a symbol of Chandigarh. While the Le Corbusier dictum—"open to receive, open to give"—is constantly bandied in the popular literature, nobody hesitates to freely interpret the Hand in their own logic. One tourist brochure calls it a giant metallic hand "of an unseen power," while another advertises it as a symbol of "Indian civilization's greedlessness and magnanimity." The administration has even constructed two more Hands at the border posts where the highway enters Chandigarh territory. Many of the city's commercial establishments have also integrated it into their own graphics. The Hand even embellishes every driver's license issued in the Union Territory (figs. 5.1, 5.2).

Graphic persuasions notwithstanding, I think it is also apposite to note that in 1980 Indira Gandhi's Congress Party adopted a new election symbol—an open hand—

that although quite distinct from that of Chandigarh, is nevertheless not that different either (fig. 5.15). It is therefore possible that some people in the Chandigarh administration may have been simply interested in ingratiating themselves with the powers that be when they aggressively went out to propagate the Open Hand in the city (plate 17).

A heroic symbol undone by the untimeliness of its own modernity and eventually realized by the whimsy of political opportunity, the Open Hand is an architect's creation whose various locations in culture weave a narrative that is as personal as it is political, and is as entrapped by the exigencies and ideals of politics as it is open to the vagaries of cultural perception. Architecture, like all other aesthetic practices, is ultimately an open sport that can be, and usually is, summarily kicked around in the larger social realm. If an architect's intentions and intuitions are critical to the conception of an architectural project, the desires and expectations, as also the circumstances of the clients who commission a project, are equally and sometimes even more critical to its understanding. And the investments of those that build and inhabit a building can tell a story that is altogether different. As such, a critical cultural historiography of architecture should not, I would contend, insist on searching for commonalities between perspectives as the only "truth" of analysis. Rather, it should simultaneously tabulate continuous and discontinuous threads with the intention of weaving a cultural narrative that helps us understand architecture as a holistic even if diffused or contradictory social praxis, and not just as a specialized aesthetic proposition. This, rather than a unitary proposition, should be the conclusion drawn from this chapter.

# Notes on Inheriting a Postcolonial Modernism

The other day a senior professor in the department stopped me in the hallway and ceremoniously presented me with a brand-new ten franc bill issued by the Swiss government. It had Le Corbusier's portrait on it, etched into history, now a symbol of the Swiss state (plates 18 and 19, see page 47). Although French by citizenship and residence, Le Corbusier was born and brought up in Switzerland. I wondered what the French would think about the Swiss reclamation of their prodigal son.

Looking carefully, I found that the background of the bill was made from superimposed layers of a distinct Le Corbusier elevation. It was the Secretariat—Chandigarh's Secretariat! I was shocked, simultaneously pleased and outraged. This was after all "my" Secretariat, or let us at least admit, the Secretariat of the government of Punjab authorized by the Indian nation-state. I could understand that I had to contend with Le Corbusier's inheritors—like the Fondation Le Corbusier—for symbolic ownership of the Capitol, but to see it usurped by another nation-state on one of its official units of exchange was outrageous. The Swiss government was clearly not commemorating an Indian building (which might have been nice); they were reclaiming what they perceived to be their own legitimate Swiss heritage.

Who owns works of architecture? Every time I went on the Capitol Esplanade as a student, there was always someone from Kansal, the village just north, bathing a buffalo, washing clothes, playing cricket, or just passing through on a bicycle or scooter. The legislators and judges never bothered to walk onto the Esplanade, since they always came and went by car from the lower level. As a consequence, in spite of the security and the official sanctity of the place, the Esplanade has become open territory for all sorts of unofficial activities. Even the security men have strung up lines to dry their laundry (fig. 6.1).

The innumerable architects who pass through Chandigarh, many of whom I escorted to the Capitol myself, generally prefer to wait patiently until the village people pass on through, so that they can get a "clean shot" of the buildings. They try to edit out the laundry from the picture frame, usually unsuccessfully, and then complain about the callous Indian government's disrespect for the great French/Swiss architect's creations.

Trademarks can be copyrighted, but the public inhabitation of architecture opens it up for appropriation by all those who want to make a claim. It is a symbolic text, simultaneously woven into as many lifeworlds as would want to make use of it. Things mesh, inevitably. In the end, therefore, I felt vindicated by the intentions of the Swiss government: if they could claim the Chandigarh Capitol as their own, surely I could claim Le Corbusier for India.

*India is an ancient land. Over the centuries there have been other new cities like Chandigarh and other prophets like Le Corbusier: Fatehpur-Sikri, Patrick Geddes, Edwin Lutyens, Golconda, Mandu. Today many of them are not perceived as foreign elements but as integral parts of the Indian landscape ...*

*India as a blotting paper. Who knows? A hundred years from now, perhaps Chandigarh will also fit seamlessly into the Punjabi ethos; perhaps it will be perceived as a famous old Indian town, and Le Corbusier will be acknowledged ... as the greatest Indian architect of them all?*

—*Charles Correa*, "Chandigarh: The View from Benares."

**Fig. 6.1** Image of Assembly with bather. (Photograph by the author)

The common perception is that a hapless Indian nation-state, clamoring to adopt modernism, begged Le Corbusier to take on Chandigarh. But the famous French architect was in fact only a circumstantial choice, an unexpected opportunity seized by a team of bureaucrats touring Europe in search of architects to complete a project that had already begun. Although Nehru, as we saw, eventually came to support Le Corbusier, it is important to note that the former was neither in favor of searching for an architect from abroad, nor did he want a specifically western modern city. Both of those decisions were in fact taken by the bureaucrats. Nehru simply wanted a city characterized by free thinking and newness.

Yet, in spite of all his rhetoric on creative thinking and articulating an original position, one of the major difficulties with the Nehruvian project of modernization was its imitation of the established practices of the developed world. While Nehru created a new foreign policy in the form of the Non-Aligned Movement, developmental practices

Fig. 6.2. Pierre Jeanneret, chief architect of Chandigarh, playfully ties P. N. Thapar, the original chief administrator of the Capitol Project, to a tree.

within India, like the Tennessee Valley Authority–inspired hydroelectric dam projects and the Soviet-style five-year plans, remained derivative and second hand. This was largely because the institutions and officers responsible for enforcing that modernity needed verifiable models of development that could be found somewhere, if not in India's past. Thus it was with Chandigarh. Chandigarh looks and feels the way it does with its neatly hierarchical sectors and plans, not because Le Corbusier and Nehru forced the reluctant inhabitants to conform, but because the officiating bureaucrats, first Fletcher and then Verma and Thapar, who conceived and cast the basic mold of Chandigarh, selected a particular image for the city. The hierarchies in the housing, the densities of the sectors, the general spread and sprawl of the city, the need for a special, symbolic administrative "head," etc., were all laid out and enforced by these officers. In the end, therefore, the fundamental character of Chandigarh's residential architecture derives from Indian bureaucratic interpretation of the English New Towns Act, derived in turn from the Garden City movement.

Beyond the Master Plan, the city's claim to modernity was settled through appearances—the city could not look colonial, or Indian, but had to look modern. This question of the "style of architecture" was made critical and imbued with symbolic purpose. P. N. Thapar, the chief administrator of the Capitol Project, emphasized it repeatedly,[1] and Maxwell Fry, Jane Drew, and Pierre Jeanneret fulfilled this modernist mandate of the city with great accomplishment. They fleshed out Le Corbusier's circulation diagram, which was intended to hold towering Unités in its pastures, with a patchwork of bungalow- and rowhouse-type dwellings.[2]

Had Mayer and Nowicki been able to complete Chandigarh, it is possible that the city might have had a more active social agenda and a more "Indian" regional aesthetic. But that proposition has only limited counterfactual value. It was Pierre Jeanneret who stayed on as the chief architect of the city until 1965, when he had to finally leave because of ill health. He is therefore quite legitimately the true chief architect of the larger city (fig. 6.2).

## Postcolonial Notes on the Capitol

What then to make of the Capitol and Le Corbusier's magisterial efforts to saturate it with an overabundance of meaning? How *was* the long distance between the East and the West ultimately negotiated in the architecture of the Capitol?

On 8 June 1967, M. S. Randhawa, the first chief commissioner of the newly created Union Territory of Chandigarh, sent a letter to André Malraux, the French minister of cultural affairs. Randhawa proposed to have the Open Hand constructed in Chandigarh as a joint Indo-French venture, a "memorial dedicated to the memory of the great architect who introduced modern architecture in India."[3] Malraux seems not to have replied.

Randhawa was not being presumptuous in approaching the famous French author and minister, since Malraux was actually a close friend of both Le Corbusier and

Nehru. Malraux in fact knew all about the Open Hand, and wrote about it in his memoirs in the context of a discussion of the differences between Eastern and Western philosophy:

> On top of [Nehru's] bookshelf, there was a large drawing by Le Corbusier: the palace of Chandigarh, surmounted by the immense Hand of Peace, looking like a cross between an emblem and a giant weathervane; and a model of the Hand, in bronze, about eighteen inches long. Le Corbusier set great store by it. Nehru, not so much. Le Corbusier had taken me round Chandigarh and had shown me the unfinished building which he had designed down to the wallpaper. In the main square, files of men and women were climbing the inclined planes, like the bowmen of Persepolis, with baskets of cement on their heads. *Here, the Assembly!* he had said to me briskly, waving his hand toward the distant Pamirs where a solitary goat was passing by. *And here* (he pointed to the roof of the law courts), *the Hand of Peace!*
>
> I thought of the glovemaker's sign in Bône, the enormous hand I had seen watching over the town like the sign of life rediscovered; and I looked at the bronze hand with its lines of fate—perhaps the fate of India.[4]

Unlike the political exigencies I have fleshed out in my chapter on the Open Hand, Malraux's narrative posits that there was a fundamental epistemological gulf between Le Corbusier and Nehru. Ultimately, Malraux suggests, they did not quite understand each other:

> In spite of sin, in spite of the devil, in spite of the absurd, in spite of the unconscious, the European thinks of himself as acting, in a world in which change is value, in which progress is conquest, in which destiny is history. The Hindu [by contrast] thinks of himself as acted upon, in a world of commemorations.[5]

Between the binary poles of acting on and being acted upon, Malraux meditates on the irreconcilability of the West and the East. The difference for him is encapsulated in the chasm between the Judeo-Christian obsession with death and the Hindu belief in the transmigration of the soul—"transmigration is always a suspended sentence, while the Christian plays out his fate once and for all."[6] "Who can kill immortality?" Malraux adduces Nehru as stating in definitive conclusion of the discussion.[7]

Without denying foundational epistemological differences, I would argue that one can account for the failure of Chandigarh's modernism in different ways that do not necessarily depend upon a fundamental epistemic chasm. Unlike Malraux's, my reading of the city and its Capitol has staged it as something like a situationist play, a drama that repeatedly twists and turns, with no real resolution in sight, and that depends on the contingencies of the actors. Nehru and Le Corbusier at times support each other, at others they do not. The city is in some parts conceived in a modern Garden City mold, and in others in one that is orientalist and rural. Nehru clearly dominates the city, but at other times it is the bureaucrats that seem to win out, while in the confines of the Capitol

Le Corbusier builds a powerless, yet conceptually powerful, private little world. The tiny little Open Hand rises on a Mediterranean beach, offers itself as the resolution of the Cold War, is checkmated by the local politics of Punjab, and yet manages to adorn every official document of both the Chandigarh administration and the Le Corbusier foundation.

Rather than a grand explanation, I have offered a concatenation of plausible propositions, seeking not the closure of the final truth, but the opening of a room full of windows offering differing ways of looking at the same picture. In the process, I have attempted to reinstate some of the losing voices in Chandigarh's history, those that are not heard so often or at least not so well. I would count Nehru's opposition to foreign architects and to the "Anglo-Saxon" predilections of the bureaucrats, as well as Le Corbusier's poignant identification with the rural peasant, as amongst those.[8]

The English architectural historian Robin Evans once wrote that "stories of origin are far more telling of their time of telling, than of the time they claim to tell."[9] In this book I have demonstrated some of the ways in which both Le Corbusier and Nehru mythologized their perceptions of India's past. But Evans's astute observation is also relevant to my own writing on the origins of Chandigarh, my perception of the events of Chandigarh's creation. I have attempted to rewrite the history of the origins of the city's modern architecture in relationship to my own postcolonial inheritance as a second-generation Chandigarh modernist. This reading is impious and appropriative. In particular it was my goal to liquefy the frozen memory of Le Corbusier in Chandigarh, presenting him as a troubled and somewhat naïve human being, desperately struggling to convert his Indian fictions into concrete, competing for the same sphere of influence with his clients and fellow architects, all of whom had their own visions at stake. In the end, my readings have simply attempted to liberate Chandigarh from some of its older creation myths—no doubt to put new ones into circulation. In the same vein and by way of conclusion, I would like to offer one last reading of the Capitol, following a circuitous detour in the form of the recovery of a lost (both in the sense of mislaid and defeated) voice.

Speaking in Chandigarh in January 1995, at a conference entitled "Theatres of Decolonization: [Architecture] Agency [Urbanism]," Gayatri Spivak, the well-known postcolonial critic and intellectual, made a case for freeing colonial architecture from the unhappy memory of colonization. It is "laughable," she argued, to shadow-box with the "mundane movement of the European colonies upon Indian soil … in the era of economic restructuring. The contemporary hybrid Indian, a product like us of history," she contended, "has internalized the idiom of minor colonial architecture now." And this, she said, should be respected, "if respect for the representative Indian citizen of today is the fundamental goal of decolonization."[10]

In that same presentation, however, Spivak discarded modernism in her astonishment about the "obstinate lingering of *guruvada*,[11] worn like a badge of honor by Le Corbusier's associates." Modernism, "Nehru's planned hybridity," as Spivak put it, was a failure because it did not "put decolonization on stage." A failure, by implication, should not qualify as a badge of honor:

> Nehru invited Le Corbusier to build Chandigarh as a staging of decolonization, but the gesture itself was part of the script: the West on tap rather than on top. The First Five Year Plan sought to supplement rural India with that Nehruvian countervision: heavy industry and urbanization. And the invitation to Le Corbusier was part of that countervision: triumphalist construction of the new nation as hybrid. It is an irony of history that that planned hybridity did not work because of a failure in the transfer of idiom (not a failure of translation) …
>
> For Chandigarh was spoilt in the fault line of *guruvada*. One of the most astonishing things at the [Chandigarh] Conference was the obstinate lingering of *guruvada*, worn like a badge of honor by Le Corbusier's associates. *Guruvada* has certainly led to spectacular expertise in India; and by other names elsewhere. But the "responsibility" of the master-disciple relationship—the critical embrace—did not come off when called upon to put decolonization on stage.[12]

Nehruvian modernization never managed to put decolonization on stage. In spite of all symbols and plans, India still remains poverty-stricken with an ever-widening gulf between rich and poor. Nor would I contest the commonplace critique that the Chandigarh Capitol, both as institution and symbol, has not fulfilled its officially stated aspiration to be a symbol of the nation's faith in the future. On the contrary, Chandigarh today is emerging from a prolonged political siege—cordoned off by layers of barbed wire and backed up by sand-bags and the military, the Capitol symbolizes and is the very site of a beleaguered state.

In Spivak's critique of Nehruvian modernization, the critical issue is the question of the ethics of representation, both in the political sense of "speaking for" and in the aesthetic sense of re-presenting, "saying anew."[13] The call to modernity, especially in architecture and urban planning, did not usher in a revolutionary modern era as Nehru had hoped, because the people, the representative citizens, were not involved in the process, were not properly represented. Laurie Baker, the English architect who has practiced on a small scale in southern India for the last forty-odd years, voiced this simply by starting a speech (sponsored by the Indian Institute of Architects) on the topic "Architecture and the People" with the following words:

> The subject given to me is Architecture and the People. Did the promoters mean *the* people, or could they have said architecture and People? Saying *the* People implies that we architects are in one category and the people are in another.[14]

In India, the architects and planners are considered "professionals," and in terms of our colonial and modern legacy, they *are* in one category, and the people in another. That is what it means to be professional, i.e., to be not untrained. Consequently, modernism, not only architectural but also economic and institutional modernism, certainly produced a great deal of professional expertise, but failed to stage the decolonization of India because its elitist, top-down framing never enabled it to gain the legitimacy to represent properly, to speak for, the people in whose name it was exercised. The failure here was *not* one of translation, as Spivak points out, but one of the *transfer* of idiom.

The last point needs to be stressed. If modernism failed in India, it was not because it was "Western," or because it relied on universal ideals. It failed because it relied on the ideological conviction that an enlightened elite could lead the rest of the populace simply by relying on the strength of symbolic demonstration. Rethinking modernism thus cannot be done through a palliative ethno-aestheticism, such as a "critical regionalism," because the problem was not fundamentally aesthetic; i.e., the problem was not that of a lack of *translation* of idiom—people accept the foreign quite easily as their own if it is useful and beneficial to them. Rather the problem was the lack of the *transfer* of idiom. Modernism came top-down. Although heroic, it proved to be only a mitigation of India's problems. We have therefore to rethink modernism, its successes and failures, as fundamentally interwoven with the larger political and ethical textile of the nation-state and its subjects.

What then, if any, would be the significance from this perspective of the blocked-off, untranslated idiom of the Capitol and its covert Rousseauesque garden of Eden?

The village of Kansal just north of Le Corbusier's Capitol still exists, and indeed it is the people of Kansal who traverse the Capitol Esplanade most often—it is a shortcut on their way to work in the city—and their children play cricket in its fields, while their cows and buffaloes receive leisurely baths in its reflecting pools (fig. 6.3, plate 20). Perhaps this *was* the intended destiny of the Capitol, since the people of Kansal, in Le Corbusier's cosmogony, were its idealized occupants. Perhaps, then, this is Le Corbusier's vision come home to roost.

Such a reading would not be inappropriate from the Nehruvian nation-state's point of view. The Capitol houses the institutions of democracy that are inherited from the British and imported from the West—the Parliamentary Assembly, the High Courts of the state, and the Secretariat. And Rousseau's noble savage *is* after all the agent of democracy valorized by the Indian state.

This reading arrives at the nexus of a Nehruvian-Corbusian vision, yet not by way of a happy symbiosis of symbols of western industrial modernization with the manually farming villagers of India. I am not, in other words, proposing that Chandigarh's modern architecture symbolized the fully industrialized futuristic desires of the backward Indian farmer who currently labors the plow by hand and oxen. A casual visitor may interpret the Capitol as such, and indeed that may also have been the agenda of the Nehruvian nation-state. This reading, superficial and symptomatic in its efforts, embodies yet another instance of the state's attempt to verify (make into truth) its ideological narratives through the authoritative transformation of architecture. By contrast, my reading arrives at the crossroads of modernity and the village farmer, of West and East, through the unexpected happenstance that Le Corbusier's primitivistic conception of the Indian peasant as a noble savage, is also the idealized agent of the Indian nation-state's democratic faith.

The noble savage of Chandigarh, of course, still constitutes a displaced vision born, as some might say, in the orientalizing plains of France. The Capitol as a redemptive mytho-poetic landscape is no doubt derived from concepts located deep in the heart of western metaphysics. But that by itself is no reason to disparage quickly its claims to nobility on the symbolic plains of Chandigarh. One cannot hold out much hope that its complex iconography, deeply personal to Le Corbusier, *as such* successfully translates for anyone, far less the rural peasantry of the Capitol village. But the question, again, is not one of translation but one of occupation and appropriation. The grafting of an idiom from one plain to another, accompanied by its unexpected blooming, is one of *the* quintessential characteristics of postcolonial India, exemplified, for example, by the unbridled flourishing of English in everyday parlance, in governance, and in literature in India.

The quotation that I have used as the epigraph of this chapter is by Charles

Fig. 6.3. Chandigarh's Open Hand monument, with a game of cricket in the foreground. (Photograph by the author)

Correa, a well-known Bombay-based architect, who characterized Chandigarh as being born "without umbilical cord." It ends his article provocatively entitled "Chandigarh: The View from Benares" originally published in the *Le Corbusier Archives*. Benares, at least in the popular imagination, must be one of the most "Indian" cities. Presented as the "View from Benares," the speculation that "perhaps … Le Corbusier will be acknowledged … as the greatest *Indian* architect of them all," is pregnant with irony. But the logical sequence it follows seems acceptable. Fatehpur Sikri, Golconda, and Mandu must have been foreign to their times, but are today woven flawlessly into the Indian fabric. Will that then also be the fate of Chandigarh?

Indeed, if one wanted, one could already see how the "Indianization" of Chandigarh might happen and how it is already happening. Prakash talks of how the Capitol buildings can be revered as old Indian temples,[15] and Correa suggests that Le Corbusier thought of architecture as a sacred undertaking; an idea that resonates well in the Indian mind.[16] Perhaps, then, Correa's suggestion that just as "India was lucky to get Le Corbusier; Le Corbusier was lucky to get India," is on the mark.[17] In which case his characterization of Le Corbusier as the "greatest Indian architect" might become acceptable.

## Chapter 1

1  Born Charles Edouard Jeanneret, Le Corbusier took on his present name in 1921 to sign his paintings. After 1929, he completely dropped Jeanneret and was known only as Le Corbusier.

2  Based on personal interview with the author. A description of this encounter can also be found in Aditya Prakash, "Working with the Master," *InsideOutside* (April–May 1984): 46-50.

3  Vikram Bhatt and Peter Scriver, *After the Masters* (Ahmedabad, India: Mapin Publications; Middletown, NJ: Grantha Corp., 1990).

4  About 6.2 million Muslims left India for Pakistan, and about 7.5 million Hindus and Sikhs came the other way. Ravi Kalia, *Chandigarh: In Search of an Identity* (Carbondale and Edwardsville: Southern Illinois University Press, 1987), p. 1. Kalia's book is based on extensive primary research and is currently the most authoritative source for facts and information on Chandigarh.

5  For a compelling account of the events of partition, see Larry Collins and Dominique Lapierre, *Freedom at Midnight* (New York: Simon and Schuster, 1975).

6  Nehru's letter to the Chief Minister is dated September 1949 and concerns latter-day waffling by the State Government on issues of financing. It nevertheless conveys Nehru's opinion from the very beginning. Quoted in Kalia, *Chandigarh*, p. 10.

7  According to a personal interview with Ravi Kalia; see Ibid., p. 3.

8  Interview with Aditya Prakash, September 1999. Also quoted in Aditya Prakash, *Reflections on Chandigarh* (New Delhi: Navyug Traders, 1983), p. 1.

9  One of the survey maps in the Chandigarh Museum shows that there was a village named Chandigarh on this site.

10  Quoted by Norma Evenson in *Chandigarh* (Berkeley: University of California Press, 1966). This quote, found on every little pamphlet on Chandigarh, seems to exist only in the oral history of the city. I could not locate an official source for it, although I presume Nehru spoke it at one of the many times he came to inaugurate the new projects of the city. For a succinct general introduction to Chandigarh's history and planning principle, see "An Introduction to Chandigarh" in Prakash 1983. For a detailed description of Chandigarh's political history, see Kalia, *Chandigarh* (1987).

11  Fondation Le Corbusier, Paris (henceforth referred to as FLC), File P2–13, p. 292. The Fondation Le Corbusier is the official archive of Le Corbusier's estate; the file and page numbers follow the Fondation's system of cataloguing the material in their possession.

12  Such as the Indian Institute of Technologies that ended up exporting its engineers to the United States in large numbers.

13  FLC, P2–13, p. 298.

14  This stereotype justified the contradictory proposition that colonization was justifiable as the spread of Enlightenment principles. The contradiction, however, was productive, as it permitted the voicing and the sublation of the Orient, as it legitimized colonization as not only the proper representation of the Orient but also as its modernization through intercourse with the colonizers, the express purpose of Empire, undertaken for the Orient's own good.

15  I argue this fully in chapter 3. But for an insightful assembly of the argument see Adolf M. Vogt, *Le Corbusier, the Noble Savage* (Cambridge, MA: MIT Press, 1998).

16  From *Le Corbusier Sketchbooks*, Vols. 1–4 (New York and Cambridge, MA: The Architectural History Foundation and MIT Press, in collaboration with the Fondation Le Corbusier, 1981), Vol. 2, Sketch no. 448–449. The sketch books, seventy in number in the original, have been published

in this edition as follows: Vol. 1: 1914–1948, Vol. 2: 1950–1954, Vol. 3: 1954–1957, and Vol. 4: 1957–1964.

These sketchbooks will be one of my main resources in this book. All references will be to this edition, and volume and sketch numbers only will be noted in parentheses in the text as follows: (Volume number#Sketch number). All English translations from the French are, unless otherwise noted, from the notes by Françoise de Franclieu that accompany each volume.

17 Quoted from Madhu Sarin, *Urban Planning in the Third World* (London: Mansell Publishing Limited, 1982), p. 44.

18 Jawaharlal Nehru, "Mr. Nehru on Architecture," *Urban and Rural Planning Thought* 2.2 (April 1959), p. 49.

19 FLC, P2–13, p. 254.

20 Nehru 1959, p. 49.

21 Le Corbusier: *The Final Testament of Père Corbu*, ed. and trans. Ivan Zaknic (New Haven, CT: Yale University Press, 1995), p. 124.

22 Le Corbusier, *Last Works*, ed. Willy Boesiger (London: Thames and Hudson, 1970), p. 174. In his sketchbook he once noted: "Every morning I awaken in the skin of an imbecile— in the evening it gets better." (3#966) One is not sure which was more important: waking up an "imbecile," or getting "better."

23 Modernisms that are "symmetrical but irreducibly different," as Gayatri Spivak once put it. Spivak, "The Politics of Translation," in *Destabilizing Theory* (Stanford: Stanford University Press,1992).

24 See Evenson, *Chandigarh*, p. 196; Sarin, *Urban Planning in the Third World*, p. 197; and Kalia, *Chandigarh*, p. 198.

25 William J. R. Curtis, *Modern Architecture Since 1900* (Oxford: Phaidon, 1982), pp. 194–97. The correlation of the Altas Museum and the Assembly first appears in Colin Rowe and Fred Koetter, *Collage City* (Cambridge, MA: MIT Press, 1978).

26 Curtis 1982, p. 277.

27 William J. R. Curtis, *Le Corbusier* (New York: Rizzoli, 1986), p. 198.

28 This has been elaborated by Gayatri Spivak, noted postcolonial critic and philosopher. In her essay "Acting Bits/Identity Talk," Spivak argues for the necessity of remaining attentive to the manner in which institutions in culture are subtended by the instituting, i.e., by the staging of culture. "Institutions in Culture," Spivak underlines, "must precomprehend [the] … instituting of culture, not simply as a chronologically prior event but as a philosophically subtending layer" (1992, p. 775).

29 For another elaboration of this argument, see Vikramaditya Prakash, "Abstraction: A Cultural Idea," *Column 5* 12 (1998): 28–31.

30 The use of other aesthetic devices in other cultures—as for instance the ideas of "rasa" or "shunyata" in the Hindu-Buddhist traditions— not only escapes Curtis, but may be entirely inconceivable from within his historiographical framework.

31 For this discussion, see especially chapter 4.

32 I refer, of course, not only to *Orientalism* (New York: Pantheon, 1978), but also to Said's later work, particularly *Culture and Imperialism* (New York: Knopf, 1993). There is also an excellent issue of *Design Book Review* (Summer/Fall 1993), dedicated to orientalism and architectural historiography.

33 The point becomes clear when one realizes that the "West" was also produced in this process as an Orientalist stereotype, as the Other's Other.

34 I have argued this fully in my article "Identity Production in Postcolonial Indian Architecture: Re-Covering What We Never Had," *Postcolonial Space(s)*, ed. N. B. Nalbantoglu and C.T. Wong (New York: Princeton Architectural Press, 1997), pp. 39–52.

35 I developed this argument earlier in my "Identity Production in (Post)Colonial 'Indian' Architecture: Hegemony and Its Discontents in C19 Jaipur" (Ph.D. diss., Cornell University, 1994), which has been cited by Mark Jarzombek in "Prolegomena to Critical Historiography," *Journal of Architectural Education* 52.4 (May 1999): 197–206.

36  A context may be simply or uncritically represented in the design, or it may be transformed in accordance with the logics of the design. This relationship may be, as Dominick LaCapra puts it, "symptomatic, critical or potentially transformative." Dominick LaCapra, *History*, *Politics and the Novel* (Ithaca, NY: Cornell University Press, 1987), p. 4.

37  Ultimately, "India," like "Europe," is a legal term, or better a catachresis—an empty concept-metaphor with no adequate referent in reality. This does not, however, make it any less important or critical to the description of relevant concepts of everyday life.

38  I am invoking both senses of the word "wake" here, as in a funeral but also as in the wake of a boat.

39  *Le Corbusier Archives*, vols. I–XXXII (New York and London: Garland; Paris: Fondation Le Corbusier, 1983). The volume, page number, and drawing number of each one of the drawings referred to will be included in parenthesis in the text itself as follows: (volume no.# page no.# drawing no). Note: The drawing number used will always be the one given by the Fondation Le Corbusier. This should not be confused with the original drawing number that may also be on the page, at times more prominently marked than the number given by the Fondation.

# Chapter 2

1  Charles Correa, "Chandigarh: The View from Banares." In *Le Corbusier*, ed. Allen H. Brooks (Princeton: Princeton University Press, 1987), p. 197.

2  The team of Indian architects was rarely consulted.

3  These, in fact, resulted in its peremptory dismissal in May 1952 by Jawaharlal Nehru, which was accompanied by the promulgation of president's rule.

4  *Notes recorded by Mr. A. L. Fletcher, I.C.S., O.S.D. (Capital), in the year 1948 on: (1) Planning (2) Architecture (3) Construction of Government Buildings (High Court, Secretariat, University etc.)* (henceforth referred to as *Fletcher's Notes*), p. 8, Chandigarh Archives, City Museum, Chandigarh. The files of the Chandigarh Archives are an invaluable source of information from the Indian side. Most of their holdings consist of bureaucratic files, which are of great historical value. The archives are located in an especially constructed building right next to the museum in sector 10 of the city.

5  *Fletcher's Notes*, p. 17.

6  See *Selection of the Architects and Town Planners for Chandigarh Capital.—Visit of Mr. P. N. Thapar and P. L. Verma to Europe* (henceforth referred to as *Selection of the Architects*), n.p. Chandigarh Archives.

7  Verma's reasons for the competition proposal may have been simply departmental politics, since Verma and Fletcher, the senior bureaucrats concerned with the project at this time, did not see eye to eye at all and indeed hated each other according to Aditya Prakash's recollections.

8  The C. E. (Dev.) is the Chief Engineer of Development, i.e., P. L. Verma.

9  *Fletcher's Notes*, p. 103.

10  Ibid., p. 105.

11  Ebenezer Howard, *Garden Cities of To-Morrow (Being the Second Edition of "To-Morrow: A Peaceful Path to Real Reform")* (London: S. Sonnenschein, 1902).

12  That number, however, was adjusted to

accommodate the realities of the new towns.

13   Fletcher here is quoting one of his unnamed "authorities" in a note dated 28 May 1948. *Fletcher's Notes*, p. 93.

14   All the above from *Fletcher's Notes*, pp. 120–30.

15   *Administrative files 1947–50*, Chandigarh Archives. In addition, Verma argued that Fletcher had simply underestimated the eventual population of Chandigarh because he had based his calculations on an English family size of four to five and not the Indian family size of seven to eight.

16   *Fletcher's Notes*, part II, p. 36.

17   Ravi Kalia, *Chandigarh* (Carbondale: University of Illinois Press, 1987), p. 26.

18   *Selection of the Architects*, p. 28. Nehru also recommended Otto Koenigsberger, who was developing the new towns of Bhubeneshwar, but he was not selected for the job.

19   See P. N. Thapar's report, "Expert for New Capital" in *Cabinet Sub-committee on Capital. Agenda and Minutes Etc. 1949-50* (hence-forth referred to as *Cabinet Sub-committee*), no. 2 , pp. 69–70. Chandigarh Archives.

20   The background information on Mayer is derived from Robert C. Emmett, *Guide to the Albert Mayer Papers on India in the University of Chicago Library* (Chicago: Committee on Southern Asian Studies. Southern Asia Reference Center, University of Chicago, 1977).

21   As quoted in Emmett, *Guide to the Albert Mayer Papers*, p. 4.

22   Ibid., p. 5.

23   Ibid., p. 6.

24   See Nikhil Gupta's thesis proposal, "Redevelopment of Mahatma Jyotiba Phule Market (Crawford Market), Bombay, with Conservation of Heritage Building." TVB School of Habitat Studies, New Delhi, 1995. http://www.cssnet.com/nitin/CRAWFORD.HTM

25   *Cabinet Sub-committee*, p. 244.

26   See Chris Gordon and Kist Kilian, "Chandigarh Forty Years After Le Corbusier," *Architectura & Natura Quarterly* (c.1990), p. 24.

27   See images in Gordon and Kilian, "Chandigarh Forty Years After," pp. 14–18.

28   Kalia, *Chandigarh*, p. 36

29   *Selection of the Architects*, p. 228.

30   *Œuvre complète 1946–1952*, ed. Willy Boesiger (Zürich: Verlag für Architektur, 1953), p. 114.

31   *Selection of the Architects*, pp. 26–27.

32   On 11 May 1951, Maxwell Fry wrote him a letter which Le Corbusier received in Bogota, complaining that both "Jeanneret and [Fry] were shocked by the extent to which in your letter of 25 April you had assumed the direction and responsibility for the whole affair. … There is no reason why a group of buildings should not be designed by a group of CIAM architects, but I am opposed to the idea of designing individual buildings in a group or of merely carrying out your designs." Quoted in Sarin, "Chandigarh As a Place to Live In," in *The Open Hand*, ed. Russell Warden (Cambridge, MA: MIT Press, 1977), p. 401.

33   Gordon and Kilian, "Chandigarh Forty Years After," p 14.

34   Maxwell Fry, "Le Corbusier at Chandigarh," in *The Open Hand*, ed. Russell Walden (Cambridge, MA: MIT Press, 1977), p. 354.

35   Stanislaus von Moos, *Le Corbusier, Elements of a Synthesis* (Cambridge, MA: MIT Press, 1985), p. 259.

36   The sectors of Chandigarh were designed as neighborhood units, with the pedestrian as the focus. Vehicular movement into them was carefully regulated by a hierarchy of streets (V4s–V7s) with decreasing access. They were also carefully separated by a wall from the V2s and V3s that form the grid of the city. No houses opened onto these streets.

37   It is commonplace to berate Le Corbusier for his putative love of the automobile, but, as Marshall Berman has argued, even in the 1920s Le Corbusier was ambivalent in his domestication of the automobile.

   Le Corbusier made a "Faustian pact" with the automobile, Berman argues, trading in the pleasure of singing and arguing in the streets for possibilities generated by the auto-mobile's power and speed. Marshall Berman, *All That Is Solid Melts into Air* (New York: Simon and Schuster, 1982),  pp. 165-69.

38  FLC, P2-12, p. 120.

39  Fry, "Le Corbusier at Chandigarh," pp. 358-59.

40  Le Corbusier, *Œuvre complète 1946-1952*, p. 158.

41  Le Corbusier, *Œuvre complète 1952-1957*, p. 51.

42  FLC, P2-12, p. 329.

43  *Selection of the Architects*, no page numbers (c. p. 200).

44  FLC, P2-13, pp. 35-36.

45  Ibid., p. 36.

46  *Times of India*, 12 March 1959. Photocopy in FLC, P2-13, pp. 209-210.

47  This is the term used by Le Corbusier. See *Selection of the Architects*, p. 122.

48  Le Corbusier's writings always contained disparaging remarks against bureaucrats. See, for instance, *The Final Testament of Père Corbu*:"… we live in a world of bureaucrats closed in upon themselves, incapable of making a decision." Le Corbusier. *The Final Testament of Père Corbu*, ed. and trans. Ivan Zaknic (New Haven, CT: Yale University Press, 1997), p. 85.

49  Apparently P. N. Thapar, the chief administrator, had made it clear from the very outset that there were to be no skyscrapers in Chandigarh. See Norma Evenson, *Chandigarh* (Berkeley: University of California Press, 1966), p. 78.

50  These sketches have no dates on them, but I have dated them for November 1951 since they are in the sketchbook marked "India / 1951 / 27 octobre / 28 novembre." (3#608) There is no reason to doubt the accuracy of the dates on this cover since some of the surrounding sketches are also from this period. (3#624, 660) One may note that they pre–date the drawings of December 1951 discussed above, thus indicating a certain time lag between the suggestion of an idea and its execution. I would attribute this to the gestation period that Le Corbusier talks about. "It's an animal sort of a thing. …When I get an idea, I ruminate it inside me, like cows do. And the idea starts to work, little by little, by itself. Several months later, if it's a good idea, it explodes. Other architects take up a pencil as soon as an idea comes to

them. I don't." Quoted from Jean Petit, *Le Corbusier lui-même* (Geneva: Rousseau, 1970), p. 184.

51  Le Corbusier, "The Master Plan," *Marg*. 15 (December 1961), p. 10.

## Chapter 3

1   William Curtis, *Modern Architecture Since 1900* (Oxford: Phaidon, 1982), p. 279.

2   Mogens Krustrup, *Porte email/Emaljeporten/ La porte émaillée/The enamel door* (Kobenhavn: Arkitektens Forlag, 1991), p. 153.

3   Ibid., p. 153.

4   Ibid.

5   Ibid., p. 154.

6   Krustrup, *Porte email . . .* (1991).

7   Richard Moore (1977) and Mogens Krustrup (1991), among others, have produced fascinating analyses of Le Corbusier's later post-purist paintings and sculptures as symbolic texts that interpret the mythopoetic preoccupations of the hand that made them. Moore sees them as the progressive unfolding of an alchemical duality between sun and moon, sky and earth, masculine and feminine, etc., mediated and sublimated by the alchemical/dialectic synthesis of their dividing line, that is also a vertical axis, rising upward. Krustrup further interprets the paintings as self-portraits of Le Corbusier and Yvonne, his wife, symbolized by mythological animistic forms, themselves symbolic of "higher" cosmic and natural principalities.

    Krustrup has conducted a detailed analysis of the Door, and in my text I will extract certain sections from his reading that help me to make the landscape of the Capitol cohere. The painting on the Door is closely related to the drawings published not long before the Door was made in Le Corbusier's *Le Poème de l'angle droit* (Paris: Fondation Le Corbusier, Editions Connivences, 1989).

8   Le Corbusier, "The Master Plan," *Marg.* 15 (1961): 5-19. Le Corbusier notes that "when the first drawings were being made, in 1952, in the garden of the rest-house on the road [from] Delhi to Simla, Jane Drew said; 'Corbu, why do you not set up between the edifices of the Capitol certain of the signs sometimes evoked by you which symbolize your strongest preoccupations . . .' (p. 18). That was the starting point. The monuments were installed on the drawings of the Capitol, the monuments symbols of a high preoccupation—of the major preoccupation in the mind of a constructor.
    Here in India, here, particularly in the Capitol of Chandigarh:
    —the 24 SOLAR HOURS
    —the COURSE OF THE SUN BETWEEN TWO SOLSTICES
    —the TOWER OF SHADE
    —the MODULOR."

9   They did not work though, ironically enough. The concrete gathers heat during the day and radiates it out at night.

10  The solar symbolism of the roof is crossbred with imagery of an eighteenth-century observatory in Jaipur called Janter Manter. See chapter 4 for a detailed discussion.

11  Le Corbusier (1961, p. 18) also makes a note of "solar festivals" that were supposed to be held inside the legislative chamber, a remark which remains unclear. Rumor has it that a beam of light was supposed to shine on a statue of Gandhi located strategically in the chamber on the solstices. But this has never occurred.

12  Edouard Schuré, *The Great Initiates*; trans. Gloria Rasberry (Nyack, NY: St. George Books, 1961).

13  Ibid., p. 46.

14  Ibid., p. 75.

15  Ibid., p. 122.

16  This is what Gayatri Spivak would call epistemic violence. See Spivak, "Can the Subaltern Speak?" In *Selected Subaltern Studies*, ed. Ranajit Guha and Gayatri Chakravorty Spivak (New York: Oxford University Press, 1988), pp. 3–34.

17  Paul V. Turner, *The Education of Le Corbusier* (New York: Garland Publishers, 1977), p. 24.

18  Le Corbusier, *The Final Testament of Père Corbu* (New Haven, CT: Yale University Press, 1997), p. 100.

19  Turner, *The Education of Corbusier*, p. 3. The other two were those of Cervantes and Rabelais.

20  Le Corbusier, *The Final Testament*, p. 85.

21  Le Corbusier, *Last Works*, ed. Willy Boesiger

(London : Thames and Hudson, 1970), p. 173.

22 Ibid., p. 176.

23 Ibid., p. 177. This lone sentence hangs by a thread in a prominent break in the narrative. It follows suddenly after a description of a visit by a friend and is followed immediately after the ellipses by a concluding discussion, the final denouement of the essay.

24 Quoted in Sarin, *Urban Planning in the Third World* (London: Mansell, 1982), p. 40.

25 Le Corbusier, "The Master Plan," p. 10.1.

26 Nek Chand's Rock Garden is a technically illegal incursion.

27 While the Governor's Palace no doubt would drastically help to complete the Capitol, the record shows that Le Corbusier, who rarely shied away from expressing his opinion, did not seem to greatly protest the executive decision not to realize it. He seemed to have settled much too easily and expended all his energy in having the Open Hand built.

28 Le Corbusier, *Œuvre complète 1957–1965*, p.95. Le Corbusier was fascinated by the function of water in Indian life and by the various bodies of water. He made sketches of the ponds that accompany almost every Indian village (4#203) and noted how they served to "make the village" (2#345). He carefully studied the use of water pools in the Viceroy's palace (2#399) and the Golden Temple in Amritsar (2#1052). These bodies of water were recreated as large pools in front of the High Court and Assembly. These pools were fed by the rainwater collected from the runoff from the buildings. The inverted parasol roofs of the High Court and the unbuilt Governor's Palace, in fact, seem to have been designed only to collect the water in a central trough. This trough spilled into two small pools via huge gargoyles, which were connected to the main pools by a system of channels. This system for water collection was informed by studies Le Corbusier did on the water channels of the Mughal gardens, especially the one at Pinjore.

29 Caroline Constant correctly identifies the Islamic paradise garden as a possible source of reference for the Capitol. However, she fails to note that the Islamic paradise garden is identical to the Christian garden of Eden, and proceeds to interpret the reference to the Islamic garden as symptomatic of the presence of the "East" in Le Corbusier's architecture. Le Corbusier may have also been referring to the Islamic garden, but for me, the important thing is the manner in which this allusion to Judeo-Christian-Islamic myths of origin is played out as the prophesy of modernism. Constant, "From the Virgilian Dream to Chandigarh," *Architectural Review* 181: 66–72.

30 The animals in the yellow panel are a signatory joke. They describe the team working on Chandigarh; the cock is Jeanneret, the goat Jane Drew, and the calf suckling at the goat is Maxwell Fry.

31 My interpretation is derived from Mogens Krustrup's readings of the Door (cf. Krustrup 1991).

32 See also Carolyn Merchant, "Reinventing Eden." In *Uncommon Ground: Toward Reinventing Nature*, ed. William Cronon (New York: Norton, 1995), for a related and more extensive discussion on the role of Edenic resurrection in modern Western civilization. (I am grateful to Sibel Bozdogan for this lead.)

33 Or how they are "orientalized," as Edward Said would put it.

34 Le Corbusier entered and won this competition, but was disqualified on technical grounds.

35 This is discussed in Adolf Vogt, *Le Corbusier, the Noble Savage* (Cambridge, MA: MIT Press, 1998), pp. 8–9.

36 Le Corbusier, *Precisions on the Present State of Architecture and City Planning*; trans. Edith Schreiber Aujame (Cambridge, MA: MIT Press, 1991).

37 Ibid., p. 49 (emphasis mine).

38 Quoted in Vogt, *Le Corbusier*, p. 146.

39 Ibid., pp. 148–49 (emphasis mine).

40 The set of Rousseauist ideas that were internalized by Le Corbusier, and with which I will be concerned in the following, are already Le Corbusier's own version of Rousseau's ideas. Whereas Le Corbusier's vision of the Capitol and the League of Nations project was

Edenic, that is not the case for Rousseau's state of nature as the previous quotes from the *Social Contract* show.

41 Le Corbusier, *Precisions on the Present State of Architecture*, p. 9.

42 Ibid., p. 10.

43 Ibid. "And I remember that back in 1910 the people of Pera said to me of the Turks of Stamboul [sic]: "You're crazy to go there at night; they'll kill you, they're tough.""

44 Quoted in Vogt, *Le Corbusier*, p. 300. Vogt is quoting one C. W. Jeanneret, secretary of the local College, from a schoolbook used by Le Corbusier.

45 Le Corbusier, *Precisions on the Present State of Architecture*, p. 10.

46 Paradise yesterday, paradise tomorrow, but never paradise today, to paraphrase Lewis Caroll in *Alice's Adventures in Wonderland*.

# Chapter 4

1 Aditya Prakash in an email to the author (December 1999).

2 See Caroline Constant, "From the Virgilian Dream to Chandigarh," *Architectural Review* 181 (1987).

3 Le Corbusier, *Modulor 2* (London: Faber and Faber, 1958), p. 214.

4 Ibid., pp. 214–15.

5 The Secretariat seems to be unconnected, floating like an appendage to the Assembly.

6 The sketch seems to be made from the point on the Esplanade where the arms of the cross-axis intersect, indicating a certain privilege to that spot between the Assembly and the High Court as a place for viewing the "exact" composition of the Capitol. This is where the "Martyr's Memorial" has been located, which has a ramp that does lead up to a viewing platform.

7 Le Corbusier, "The Master Plan," *Marg.* 15 (1961), p. 10.1.

8 Le Corbusier, *Modulor 2*, p. 214.

9 See Le Corbusier's two volumes on the Modulor from 1954 and 1958. Le Corbusier wrote in his final testament: "I have for 50 years been studying the chap known as "Man" and his wife and kids. I have been inspired by one single preoccupation, imperatively so; to introduce into the home the sense of the sacred; to make the home the temple of the family" (Le Corbusier, *Last Works*, ed. Willy Boesiger [London: Thames and Hudson, 1970], p. 174). I simply note this here, since a full discussion of the deep cultural sexism of that remark is beyond the purview of this analysis. For landmark feminist critiques of Le Corbusier see Beatriz Colomina, "Le Corbusier and Photography," *Assemblage* 4 (October 1987): 6–23, and Zeynep Celik, "Le Corbusier, Orientalism, Colonialism," *Assemblage* 17 (April 1992): 58–77.

10 Le Corbusier, "The Master Plan," p. 10.

11 Le Corbusier, *Modulor 2*, p. 215. (emphasis mine)

12 Ibid., pp. 210–14.

13 Orthogonal architectural drawings, in another

register, are also designed to achieve the same end. This is perhaps why architects may find his paintings more interesting than painters.

14  The section of the building, however, gives no indication that this might be so.

15  Robert Slutzky also noticed this and described it playfully as "aqueous humor." Slutzky, "Aqueous Humor," *Oppositions* 19/20 (Winter/Spring 1980): 29–51.

16  The section, by contrast, with its butterfly roof, of course, is a purposeful manifestation of gravity, like the other buildings of the Capitol.

17  Le Corbusier, *The Final Testament of Père Corbu* (New Haven, CT: Yale, 1997), p. 85. Ofcourse one can argue that the *pilotis*, in a sense, always countervailed against the "weight of things."

18  See Robin Evans, "Mies van de Rohe's Paradoxical Symmetries," *AA Files* 19 (Spring 1990): 56–68.

19  Sigmund Freud, The "Uncanny." In *Writings on Art and Literature* (Stanford: Stanford University Press, 1997), p. 213. Anthony Vidler, in *The Architectural Uncanny* (Cambridge, MA: MIT Press, 1992), has a sustained discussion of the role of the uncanny in architecture; he documents various ways in which what might be considered uncanny properties function in architecture. The way I am invoking the concept here, however, is missing from Vidler's text.

20  Freud, "'The Uncanny'," p. 221.

21  For a brief but informative discussion on catharsis and cathexis, see J. Laplanche and J. B. Pontalis, *The Language of Psychoanalysis* (New York: Norton, 1974), pp. 60–65.

22  Le Corbusier, *Modulor 2*, p. 215.

23  Adolf Vogt, *Le Corbusier, the Noble Savage* (Cambridge, MA: MIT Press, 1998), parts IV and V. The correspondences are conveyed visually in the composition of the cover of the book as well.

24  It is derived, of course, from Le Corbusier's *Unités d'habitation*, which were based on the section of an oceangoing liner.

25  There is, however, a Lake Club at its edge, and a viewing platform that extends over the water. Paradoxically, Matthew Nowicki's earlier design of the Capitol did, in fact, place it in the midst of this lake! Le Corbusier must surely have seen these drawings. Might his decision not to build on the lake itself have partially been determined by the anxiety of influence?

26  "Palais" in the original French is a much more commonplace word than the English "palaces."

27  A discussion of the "law of the meander" can be found in Le Corbusier's *Le Poeme de l'angle droit* (Paris: Fondation Le Corbusier, 1989).

28  Reported by Doshi in an interview. Balkrishna Doshi was one of Le Corbusier's Indian subordinates who was responsible for the Ahmedabad commissions. Doshi, *Le Corbusier and Louis I Kahn* (Ahmedabad: Vastu Shilpa Foundation [c.1992]), p. 2.

29  Quoted in Jaime Coll, "Structure and Play in Le Corbusier's Art Works," *AA Files* 31 (Summer 1996): 3.

30  Le Corbusier, *Creation Is a Patient Search* (New York: Praeger, 1960).

31  Discussed in Coll, "Structure and Play," p. 7.

32  Ibid.

33  The earliest drawings of the Assembly are from 1951, and the final design was ready in 1957. The building itself was completed in 1962. Its basic function was to house the assembly chambers of the two houses of the Punjab legislature. These were the "lower" and "upper" houses, which were modeled on the British parliamentary system. Contrary to what the titles suggest, the "lower" house was the more powerful of the two, since it was empowered to legislate. The "upper" house was basically an advisory body. The other functional requirement of this building was to provide office space.

34  Le Corbusier was considering to use real arches in the Assembly. (3#26) The arches of the High Court, however, were "false" in that they were suspended from the ceiling.

35  Doshi, *Le Corbusier and Louis I Kahn*, p. 7.

36  Le Corbusier, *Œuvre complète 1957–1965*, ed. Willy Boesiger (Zurich: Verlag für Architektur, 1965), p. 80.

37 The entrance portal was also changed substantially. In section it was still in the shape of a wing, but the arches were replaced by pylons. Le Corbusier considered two compositions for these pylons. In the first two, V-shaped pylons were set in the bays created by three tapering columns. These V-shaped pylons remind one of the armature that supports a plane on its wheels. (22#114#2895) And in the second, the V-shaped pylons were replaced by flat pylons that taper towards their edges. The flat sides face the Esplanade, so that if seen from there they look like aircraft wings would if seen from on top. (22#186#3035)

38 Le Corbusier, *Œuvre complète 1957–1965*, p. 80.

39 For a full discussion see Sigmund Freud, *The Interpretation of Dreams* (Cutchogue, NY: Buccaneer Books, 1985).

40 Le Corbusier calls the Governor's Palace the quintessential "Home of Man" in *Œuvre complète 1952–1957*, p. 102.

# Chapter 5

1 Rajneesh Wattas, "The Open Hand," *Architecture + Design* (July/August 1985): 10.

2 Vikramaditya Prakash, "Letter to the Editor," *Architecture + Design* (September/October 1985): 13.

3 FLC, P2–13, p. 286.

4 Le Corbusier, *Last Works*, ed. Willy Boesiger (London: Thames and Hudson, 1970), p. 189.

5 Le Corbusier's speech is reproduced in the appendix to Mogens Krustrup, *Porte email …*, Appendix D9 (Kobenhavn: Arkitektens Forlag, 1991).

6 Mary P. Sekler, "Le Corbusier, Ruskin, the Tree, and the Open Hand." In *The Open Hand*, ed. Russell Walden (Cambridge, MA: MIT Press, 1977), pp. 42–95.

7 Reproduced in von Moos, *Le Corbusier* (Cambridge, MA: MIT Press, 1985), p. 110. The drawing that represents the idea in Kenneth Frampton's *Modern Architecture: A Critical History* (New York: Thames and Hudson, 1992), leaves out the hand, reducing the character of agency of Le Corbusier's proposition, leaving only the idea of modularity.

8 Le Corbusier, *Œuvre compléte 1946–1952* (Zurich: Verlag für Architektur, 1953), p. 152.

9 Reproduced in Krustrup, *Porte email …*, fig. 121.

10 Le Corbusier, *The Final Testament of Père Corbu* (New Haven, CT: Yale University Press, 1997), p. 97.

11 Ibid., p. 14.

12 Ibid., p. 86.

13 Le Corbusier, *Œuvre compléte 1946–1952*, p. 155.

14 Ibid.

15 Le Corbusier's *Nivola Albums* (Paris: Fondation Le Corbusier [c. 1950–1960]), *Nivola 1*, pp. 5–47. They are dated onwards from Bogota, February 1950. This is the album that also contains the critical sketch that records Le Corbusier's decision to let the hyperbolic paraboloid project through the roof of the Assembly.

16 Le Corbusier, "The Master Plan," *Marg.* 15 (1961), p. 10.

17 Le Corbusier, *The Final Testament*, p. 176.

18 FLC, P2–13, p. 253.

19 Ibid.

20 Ibid., p. 254.

21 Jawaharlal Nehru, "Speech to Bandung Conference Political Committee, 1955." In *The Asian-African Conference*, ed. G. M. Kahim (Ithaca, NY: Cornell University Press, 1956), pp. 64–72.

22 FLC, P2–13, p. 36.

23 J. Nehru, "Mr. Nehru on Architecture," *Urban and Rural Planning Thought* 2.2 (April 1959), p. 49.

24 Had Nehru accepted the Hand as Le Corbusier offered it, would the latter have been happy to accept it as a symbol of the Non Aligned Movement? Since this is a counterfactual question, it is difficult to conclude anything with certainty, but I suspect that Le Corbusier was so keen to have his ideas accepted that he would have grasped any opportunity to have the Hand built as a prominent international political symbol.

25 Probably inspired by Marcel Breuer's work at the Grand Coulee Dam in eastern Washington.

26 Le Corbusier, *Last Works*, pp. 158–61.

27 I am grateful to M. Ijlal Muzaffer for uncovering much of what follows.

28 This is exemplified by a popular saying of the time: "The Hindus got Hindustan, the Muslims got Pakistan, what did the Sikhs get?" Quoted in Harjot S. Oberoi, "From Punjab to 'Khalistan,'" *Pacific Affairs* 60. s1 (1987): 26–41.

29 For a general discussion leading up to the division of Punjab in 1966, see Paul Brass, *Language, Religion and Politics in North India* (Cambridge: Cambridge University Press, 1974), pp. 277–336. For a discussion of the social and economic effects of the new canal projects on different areas of Punjab and their relationship to Punjab's political crisis, see Murray J. Leaf, "The Punjab Crisis," *Asian Survey* 25.5 (May 1985): 476–77. Though the second wave of agricultural reforms beginning in the early 1960s, the so-called *green revolution*, led Punjab to a new era of economic prosperity, it nevertheless could not pacify the grievance of an unequal share of power, resources, and costs that marred the egalitarian ideals represented by Bhakra and its related projects. For a detailed discussion of Punjab's continuing political crisis and its relationship to the proceeding Nehruvian agricultural reforms, see Leaf 1985; Hamish Telford, "The Political Economy of Punjab," *Asian Survey* 32.11 (November 1992): 976–81; Paul Brass, "Socio-Economic Aspects of the Punjab Crisis," *Punjab Journal of Politics* 13.1–2 (1989): 13–14; Sharanjit S. Dhillon, "Technological Change and Distribution of Gains in Agriculture," *Studies in Punjab Economy*, ed. R. S. Johar and J. S. Khanna (Amritsar: Guru Nanak Dev University, 1983), p. 423; and S. S. Grewal and P. R. Rangi, "Imbalances in Growth of Punjab Agriculture," *Studies in Punjab Economy*, ed. R. S. Johar and J. S. Khanna (Amritsar: Guru Nanak Dev University, 1983), p. 53.

30 Interview with Aditya Prakash, 1990.

31 Cf. memo dated 18 January 1974, *Official Papers of the Office of the Chief Architect. Chandigarh Administration. "The Open Hand"* (Chandigarh Archives, City Museum, Chandigarh), p. 110.

# Chapter 6

1   As recalled in interviews by Aditya Prakash. Le Corbusier also notes that the "style" of architecture was very important for Thapar. See FLC, P2–12, p. 120.

2   Kiran Joshi has recently published a documentary book on the architecture of Fry, Drew, and Jeanneret. Joshi, *Documenting Chandigarh* (Ahmedabad: Mapin, 1999).

3   In "The Open Hand," letter dated 8 June 1967 in the *Official Papers of the Office of the Chief Architect*. Chandigarh Administration, Chandigarh.

4   André Malraux, *Anti-memoirs* (New York: Holt, Rinehart, and Winston, 1968), p. 231.

5   Ibid., p. 230.

6   Ibid.

7   Ibid., p. 231.

8   More archival and anthropological work will, of course, have to be done before one can claim to have made heard more subaltern voices such as those of the rural peasants themselves, who still use the Capitol Esplanade for their daily needs.

9   Robin Evans, "Mies van der Rohe's Paradoxical Symmetries," *AA Files* 19 (Spring 1990), p. 67.

10  Quoted from an original transcript of a presentation made on 8 January 1995. These comments were edited out by Spivak in the subsequent publication "City, Country, Agency," in *Proceedings of Theatres of Decolonization*, ed. Vikramaditya Prakash (Seattle: College of Architecture and Urban Planning, University of Washington, 1997), but I include them here to share their insight.

11  Literally translated as "teacher-worship."

12  Spivak, "City, Country, Agency," p. 3.

13  This distinction is made by Spivak in "Can the Subaltern Speak?" in *Selected Subaltern Studies*, ed. Ranajit Guha and G. C. Spivak (New York: Oxford, 1988), p. 275.

14  In Gautam C. Bhatia, *Laurie Baker* (New Delhi: Viking, 1991), p. 246.

15  Aditya Prakash, *Chandigarh* (Chandigarh: Chandigarh Administration, 1980), p. 45.

16  Charles Correa, "Chandigarh," in *Le Corbusier*, ed. Allen H. Brooks (Princeton: Princeton University Press, 1987), p. 201.

17  Ibid.

# CHRONOLOGY

08/1947      Indian Independence from British Rule.

10/1949      Albert Mayers's master plan for Chandigarh.

11/1950      Le Corbusier commissioned to design Chandigarh.

02/1951      Le Corbusier's first trip to India.

09/1951      Beginning of work on the Assembly.

10/1951      First presentation drawings of the Assembly.

03/1952      Early plans of the Capitol.

06/1952      Plan of the Capitol with dune.

10/1953      Formal opening of Chandigarh by Prime Minister Nehru.

03/1954      Plan of the Capitol with hills framing the Assembly.

10/1955      Second set of presentation drawings of the Assembly.

02/1956      Final plan of the Capitol.

[?]/1957      Final design of the Assembly.

04/1962      Opening of the Assembly building.

04/1964      Le Corbusier's twenty-third and last trip to India.

Akbar, M. J. *Nehru, the Making of India*. London and New York: Viking Penguin, 1988.

Berman, Marshall. *All That Is Solid Melts into Air: The Experience of Modernity*. New York: Simon and Schuster, 1982.

Bhatia, Gautam C. *Laurie Baker*. New Delhi: Viking, 1991.

Bhatt, Vikram, and Peter Scriver. *After the Masters: Contemporary Indian Architecture*. Ahmedabad: Mapin Publications; Middletown, NJ: Grantha, 1990.

Brass, Paul. *Language, Religion and Politics in North India*. Cambridge: Cambridge University Press, 1974.

—— "Socio-Economic Aspects of the Punjab Crisis." *Punjab Journal of Politics* 13.1–2 (1989): 13–14.

Celik, Zeynep. "Le Corbusier, Orientalism, Colonialism." *Assemblage* 17 (April 1992): 58–77.

Chakravarty, Suhash. "Architecture and Politics in the Construction of New Delhi." *Architecture + Design* 2.2 (January/February 1986): 76–93.

"Chandigarh Forty Years After Le Corbusier." ANQ Document. *Architectura & Natura Quarterly*. Amsterdam, c.1991.

Coll, Jaime. "Structure and Play in Le Corbusier's Art Works." *AA Files* 31 (Summer 1996): 3–14.

Collins, Larry, and Dominique Lapierre. *Freedom at Midnight*. New York: Simon and Schuster, 1975.

Colomina, Beatriz. "Le Corbusier and Photography." *Assemblage* 4 (October 1987): 6–23.

Constant, Caroline. "From the Virgilian Dream to Chandigarh." *Architectural Review* 181 (January 1987): 66–72.

Correa, Charles. "Chandigarh: The View from Banares." In *Le Corbusier*, ed. Allen H. Brooks, pp. 197–202. Princeton: Princeton University Press, 1987.

Curtis, William J. R. *Modern Architecture Since 1900*. Oxford: Phaidon, 1982.

—— *Le Corbusier: Ideas and Forms*. New York: Rizzoli, 1986.

—— "L'Ancien dans le moderne." In *Architecture en Inde*. Commissioners: Raj Rewal, Jean-Louis Veret, and Ram Sharma. Paris: Electa Moniteur, 1985.

Dhillon, Sharanjit S. "Technological Change and Distribution of Gains in Agriculture." In *Studies in Punjab Economy*, ed. R. S. Johar and J. S. Khanna, p. 423. Amritsar: Guru Nanak Dev University, 1983.

Doshi, Balkrishna. *Le Corbusier and Louis I Kahn: The Acrobat and the Yogi of Architecture*. Ahmedabad: Vastu Shilpa Foundation, c.1992.

Emmett, Robert C. *Guide to the Albert Mayer Papers on India in the University of Chicago Library*. Chicago: Committee on Southern Asian Studies, Southern Asia Reference Center, University of Chicago, 1977.

Evans, Robin. "Mies van der Rohe's Paradoxical Symmetries." *AA Files* 19 (Spring 1990): 56–68.

Evenson, Norma. *Chandigarh*. Berkeley: University of California Press, 1966.

Frampton, Kenneth. *Modern Architecture: A Critical History*. New York: Thames and Hudson, 1992.

Freud, Sigmund. *The Interpretation of Dreams*. Trans. A. A. Brill. Cutchogue, NY: Buccaneer Books, 1985.

—— "The 'Uncanny.'" In *Writings on Art and Literature*, pp. 193–233. Stanford: Stanford University Press, 1997.

Fry, Maxwell. "Le Corbusier at Chandigarh." In *The Open Hand: Essays on Le Corbusier*, ed. Russell Walden, pp. 350–63. Cambridge, MA: MIT Press, 1977.

Gordon, Chris, and Kist Kilian. "Chandigarh Forty Years After Le Corbusier." *Architectura & Natura Quarterly*. Amsterdam, c. 1990.

Grewal, S. S., and P. R. Rangi. "Imbalances in Growth of Punjab Agriculture." In *Studies in Punjab Economy*, ed. R. S. Johar and J. S. Khanna, p. 53. Amritsar: Guru Nanak Dev University, 1983.

Havell, E. B. *The Ancient and Medieval Architecture of India: A Study of Indo-Aryan Civilization*. London: John Murray, 1915.

Howard, Ebenezer. *Garden Cities of To-Morrow (Being the Second Edition of "To-Morrow: A Peaceful Path to Real Reform)."* London: S. Sonnenschein, 1902.

Hussey, Christopher. *The Life of Sir Edwin Lutyens*. Woodbridge: Antique Collectors' Club, 1984.

Irving, Robert G. *Lutyens, Baker and Imperial Delhi*. New Haven, CT: Yale University Press, 1981.

Jacob, S. S. *Jeypore Portfolio of Architectural Details*. London: W. Griggs, 1890.

Jarzombek, Mark. "Prolegomena to Critical Historiography." *Journal of Architectural Education* 52.4 (May 1999): 197–206.

Jeanneret, Charles-Edouard. *Journey to the East*. Trans. Ivan Zaknic. Cambridge, MA: MIT Press, 1977.

—— *Voyage d'Orient. Carnets*. New York: Electa Rizzoli, 1988.

Joshi, Kiran. *Documenting Chandigarh: The Indian Architecture of Pierre Jeanneret, Edwin Maxwell Fry, Jane Beverly Drew*. Ahmedabad: Mapin Publications, 1999.

Kalia, Ravi. *Chandigarh: In Search of an Identity*. Carbondale and Edwardsville: Southern Illinois University Press, 1987.

Kipling, John Lockwood. "Indian Architecture of To-Day." *Journal of Indian Art* 1 (1884–86): 1–5.

Krustrup, Mogens. *Porte email/Emaljeporten/La porte émaillée/The enamel door: Le Corbusier, Palais de l'Assemblée de Chandigarh*. Kobenhavn: Arkitektens Forlag, 1991.

LaCapra, Dominick. *History, Politics and the Novel*. Ithaca, NY: Cornell University Press, 1987.

Laplanche, J, and J. B. Pontalis. *The Language of Psychoanalysis*. Trans. Donald Nicholson-Smith. New York: Norton, 1974.

Leaf, Murray J. *Song of Hope: The Green Revolution in a Punjab Village*. New Brunswick, NJ: Rutgers University Press, 1984.

——"The Punjab Crisis." *Asian Survey* 25.5 (May 1985): 476–77.

Le Corbusier. *Une Maison—Un Palais*. Paris: Crès, 1928.

—— *Œuvre complète 1938–1946*. Ed. Willy Boesiger; trans. William B. Gleckman. Zürich: Verlag für Architektur (Artemis), 1946.

—— *Œuvre complète 1946–1952*. Ed. Willy Boesiger; trans. William B. Gleckman. Zürich: Verlag für Architektur (Artemis), 1953.

—— *Nivola Albums*. Paris: Fondation Le Corbusier, c. 1950–60.

—— *The Modulor*. London: Faber and Faber, 1954.

—— *Œuvre complète 1952–1957*. Ed. Willy Boesiger; trans. William B. Gleckman. Zürich: Verlag für Architektur (Artemis), 1957.

—— *Modulor 2*. London: Faber and Faber, 1958.

—— *Creation Is a Patient Search*. Trans. James Palmes. New York: Praeger, 1960.

—— *Towards a New Architecture*. Trans. Frederick Etchells. New York: Praeger, 1960.

—— "The Master Plan." *Marg*. 15 (December 1961): 5–19.

—— *Œuvre complète 1957–1965*. Ed. Willy Boesiger; trans. William B. Gleckman. Zürich: Verlag für Architektur (Artemis), 1965.

—— *Last Works*. Ed. Willy Boesiger; trans. Henry A. Frey. London: Thames and Hudson, 1970.

—— *Le Corbusier Sketchbooks*, Vols. 1–4. Pref. André Wogensky; Intro. Maurice Besset; Notes Françoise de Franclieu. New York and Cambridge, MA: The Architectural History Foundation and MIT Press, in collaboration with the Fondation Le Corbusier, 1981.

—— *Le Corbusier Archives*. I–XXXII. Intro. Maurice Besset; Notes Françoise de Franclieu. New York and London: Garland; Paris: Fondation Le Corbusier, 1983.

—— *The City of Tomorrow*. Trans. Frederick Etchells. Cambridge, MA: MIT Press, 1986.

— *Le Poème de l'angle droit*. Paris: Fondation Le Corbusier. Editions Connivences, 1989.

—— *Precisions on the Present State of Architecture and City Planning*. Trans. Edith Schreiber Aujame. Cambridge, MA: MIT Press, 1991.

—— *Le Corbusier: The Final Testament of Père Corbu*. Ed. and trans. Ivan Zaknic. New Haven, CT: Yale University Press, 1995.

—— *The Final Testament of Père Corbu : A Translation and Interpretation of Mise au point*. Ed. and trans. Ivan Zaknic. New Haven, CT: Yale University Press, 1997.

Malraux, André. *Anti-memoirs*. Trans. Terence Kilmartin. New York: Holt, Rinehart, and Winston, 1968.

Merchant, Carolyn. "Reinventing Eden: Western Culture as a Recovery Narrative." In *Uncommon Ground: Toward Reinventing Nature*, ed. William Cronon. New York: Norton, 1995.

Metcalf, Thomas R. *An Imperial Vision: Indian Architecture and Britain's Raj*. Berkeley: University of California Press, 1989.

Moore, Richard. *Le Corbusier: Myth and Meta Architecture: The Late Period (1947–1965)*. Atlanta: Dept. of Art, Georgia State University, 1977.

Moos, Stanislaus von. "The Politics of the Open Hand: Notes on Le Corbusier and Nehru at Chandigarh." In *The Open Hand: Essays on Le Corbusier*, ed. Russell Walden, pp. 412–57. Cambridge, MA: MIT Press, 1977.

—— *Le Corbusier: Elements of a Synthesis*. Cambridge, MA: MIT Press, 1985.

Nehru, Jawaharlal. "Speech to Bandung Conference Political Committee, 1955." In *The Asian-African Conference*, ed. G. M. Kahim, pp. 64–72. Ithaca, NY: Cornell University Press, 1956.

—— "Mr. Nehru on Architecture." *Urban and Rural Planning Thought* 2.2 (April 1959): 46–49.

—— "Tryst with destiny speech." In *Penguin Book of Twentieth Century Speeches*, ed. Brian McArthur, pp. 234–37. London: Penguin, 1992.

Nilsson, Sten. *The New Capitals of India, Pakistan and Bangladesh*. Lund: Studentlitteratur, 1973.

Oberoi, Harjot S. "From Punjab to 'Khalistan': Territoriality and Metacommentary." *Pacific Affairs* 60.1 (1987): 26–41.

"Orientalism." *Design Book Review* (Summer /Fall 1993).

Pandit, Sneh. *Chandigarh*. Chandigarh: Sterling Printers, 1969.

Petit, Jean. *Le Corbusier lui-même*. Geneva: Rousseau, 1970.

Prakash, Aditya. *Chandigarh: A Presentation in Free Verse*. Chandigarh: Chandigarh Administration, 1980.

—— *Reflections on Chandigarh*. New Delhi: Navyug Traders, 1983.

—— "Working with the Master." *InsideOutside* (April/May 1984): 46-50.

Prakash, Aditya, and Vikramaditya Prakash. *Chandigarh: The City Beautiful*. Chandigarh: Abhishek Publications, 1999.

Prakash, Vikramaditya. "Letter to the Editor." *Architecture + Design* (September/October 1985): 13.

—— "Identity Production in Postcolonial Indian Architecture: Re-Covering What We Never Had." In *Postcolonial Space(s)*, ed. N. B. Nalbantoglu and C. T. Wong, pp. 39–52. New York: Princeton Architectural Press, 1997.

—— "Listening to the Subaltern: The Ethics of Professional Work, or Notes Towards the Pedagogy of the India Studio." In *City Space + Globalization*, ed. Hemalata C. Dandekar. Ann Arbor: College of Architecture and Urban Planning, University of Michigan, 1998.

—— "Abstraction: A Cultural Idea." *Column 5* 12 (1998): 28–31.

—— "Identity Production in (Post)Colonial 'Indian' Architecture: Hegemony and Its Discontents in C19 Jaipur." Ph.D. diss., Cornell University, 1994.

Prasad, Susand. "Le Corbusier in India." *Architecture + Design* 3.6 (September/October 1987): 14–19.

Rowe, Colin. *The Mathematics of an Ideal Villa and Other Essays.* Cambridge, MA: MIT Press, 1985.

Rowe, Colin, and Fred Koetter. *Collage City*. Cambridge, MA: MIT Press, 1978.

Rykwert, Joseph. *On Adam's House in Paradise: The Idea of the Primitive Hut in Architectural History.* New York: Museum of Modern Art, New York Graphic Society, 1972.

Said, Edward. *Orientalism*. New York: Pantheon, 1978.

—— *Culture and Imperialism*. New York: Knopf, 1993.

Sarin, Madhu. "Chandigarh as a Place to Live In." In *The Open Hand: Essays on Le Corbusier*, ed. Russell Walden, pp. 374–411. Cambridge, MA: MIT Press, 1977.

—— *Urban Planning in the Third World: The Chandigarh Experience*. London: Mansell Publishing Limited, 1982.

Schuré, Edouard. *The Great Initiates. A Study of the Secret History of Religions*. Trans. Gloria Rasberry. Nyack, NY: St. George Books, 1961.

Sekler, Mary P. "Le Corbusier, Ruskin, the Tree, and the Open Hand." In *The Open Hand: Essays on Le Corbusier*, ed. Russell Walden, pp. 42–95. Cambridge, MA: MIT Press, 1977.

Serenyi, Peter. "Timeless but of Its Time: Le Corbusier's Architecture in India." In *Le Corbusier*, ed. H. Allen Brooks. Princeton, NJ: Princeton University Press, 1987.

Shohat, Ella, and Robert Stam. *Unthinking Eurocentrism: Multiculturalism and the Media*. New York: Routledge, 1995.

Slutzky, Robert. "Aqueous Humor." *Oppositions* 19/20 (Winter/Spring 1980): 29–51.

Spivak, Gayatri C. "The Politics of Translation." In *Destabilizing Theory: Contemporary Feminist Debates*, ed. M. Barrett and A. Stanford Phillips. Stanford: Stanford University Press, 1992.

—— "Acting Bits/Identity Talk." *Critical Inquiry* 18.4 (Summer 1992): 770–803.

—— "Can the Subaltern Speak?" In *Selected Subaltern Studies*, ed. Ranajit Guha and Gayatri Chakravorty Spivak, pp. 3–34. New York: Oxford University Press, 1988.

—— "City, Country, Agency." In *Proceedings of Theatres of Decolonization: [Architecture] Agency [Urbanism]*, ed. Vikramaditya Prakash. Seattle: Office of the Dean, College of Architecture and Urban Planning, University of Washington, 1997.

Telford, Hamish. "The Political Economy of Punjab: Creating Space for Sikh Militancy." *Asian Survey* 32.11 (November 1992): 976–81.

Turner, Paul V. *The Education of Le Corbusier*. New York: Garland Publishers, 1977.

Vidler, Anthony. *The Architectural Uncanny: Essays in the Modern Unhomely*. Cambridge, MA: MIT Press, 1992.

Vogt, Adolf M. *Le Corbusier, the Noble Savage: Toward an Archaeology of Modernism*. Cambridge, MA: MIT Press, 1998.

Wattas, Rajneesh. "The Open Hand." *Architecture + Design* (July–August 1985): 10.

Young, Robert. *White Mythologies.* New York: Routledge, 1995.

# ILLUSTRATION CREDITS

Permission to reproduce the illustrations in this book is gratefully acknowledged.

## Plates

1: Navneet Saxena
2, 6, 7, 9, 10, 15, 17, 20: Author's Collection
3, 4: Chandigarh Museum Archives
5, 8, 16: Artists Rights Society/Foundation
     Le Corbusier
11, 12, 13, 14: CAUP Slide Collection, University
     of Washington
20: Swiss Government

## Chapter 1

**Fig. 1.1**: Author
**Fig. 1.2**: CAUP Slide Collection, University
     of Washington
**Fig. 1.3**: Author
**Fig. 1.4**: Author
**Fig. 1.5**: Chandigarh Museum Archives
**Fig. 1.6**: Phaidon Press LTD

## Chapter 2

**Fig. 2.1**: Chandigarh Museum Archives
**Fig. 2.2**: Chandigarh Museum Archives
**Fig. 2.3**: Chandigarh Museum Archives
**Fig. 2.4**: Chandigarh Museum Archives
**Fig. 2.5**: MIT Press
**Fig. 2.6**: Artist's Rights Society/Fondation
     Le Corbusier
**Fig. 2.7**: Artist's Rights Society/Fondation
     Le Corbusier
**Fig. 2.8**: Artist's Rights Society/Fondation
     Le Corbusier
**Fig 2.9**: Artist's Rights Society/Fondation
     Le Corbusier

## Chapter 3

**Fig. 3.1**: Artist's Rights Society/Fondation
     Le Corbusier
**Fig 3.2**: Artist's Rights Society/Fondation
     Le Corbusier
**Fig. 3.3**: Artist's Rights Society/Fondation
     Le Corbusier
**Fig. 3.4**: Artist's Rights Society/Fondation
     Le Corbusier
**Fig. 3.5**: Artist's Rights Society/Fondation
     Le Corbusier
**Fig. 3.6**: Artist's Rights Society/Fondation
     Le Corbusier
**Fig 3.7**: Artist's Rights Society/Fondation
     Le Corbusier
**Fig. 3.8**: Artist's Rights Society/Fondation
     Le Corbusier
**Fig. 3.9**: Artist's Rights Society/Fondation
     Le Corbusier

## Chapter 4

**Fig. 4.1**: Chandigarh Museum Archives
**Fig. 4.2**: Artist's Rights Society/Fondation
     Le Corbusier
**Fig. 4.3**: Artist's Rights Society/Fondation
     Le Corbusier
**Fig. 4.4**: Artist's Rights Society/Fondation
     Le Corbusier
**Fig. 4.5**: Author
**Fig. 4.6**: Artist's Rights Society/Fondation
     Le Corbusier
**Fig. 4.7**: Artist's Rights Society/Fondation
     Le Corbusier
**Fig. 4.8**: Artist's Rights Society/Fondation
     Le Corbusier
**fig 4.9**: Artist's Rights Society/Fondation
     Le Corbusier
**Fig. 4.10**: Author
**Fig. 4.11**: Artist's Rights Society/
     Fondation Le Corbusier

**Fig. 4.12**: Artist's Rights Society/
   Fondation Le Corbusier
**Fig. 4.13**: Artist's Rights Society/
   Fondation Le Corbusier
**Fig. 4.14**: Artist's Rights Society/
   Fondation Le Corbusier
**Fig. 4.15**: Artist's Rights Society/
   Fondation Le Corbusier
**Fig. 4.16**: Artist's Rights Society/
   Fondation Le Corbusier
**Fig. 4.17**: Author
**Fig. 4.18**: CAUP Slide Collection, University
   of Washington
**Fig. 4.19**: Artist's Rights Society/
   Fondation Le Corbusier

## Chapter 5
**Fig. 5.1**: Abhishek Publications
**Fig. 5.2**: Author
**Fig. 5.3**: Artist's Rights Society/Fondation
   Le Corbusier
**Fig. 5.4**: Artist's Rights Society/Fondation
   Le Corbusier
**Fig. 5.5**: Artist's Rights Society/Fondation
   Le Corbusier
**Fig. 5.6**: Artist's Rights Society/Fondation
   Le Corbusier
**Fig. 5.7**: Artist's Rights Society/Fondation
   Le Corbusier
**Fig. 5.8**: Artist's Rights Society/Fondation
   Le Corbusier
**Fig. 5.9**: Artist's Rights Society/Fondation
   Le Corbusier
**Fig. 5.10**: Artist's Rights Society/
   Fondation Le Corbusier
**Fig. 5.11**: Artist's Rights Society/
   Fondation Le Corbusier
**Fig. 5.12**: Artist's Rights Society/
   Fondation Le Corbusier
**Fig. 5.13**: Artist's Rights Society/
   Fondation Le Corbusier
**Fig. 5.14**: Aditya Prakash
**Fig. 5.15**: Architectura & Natura Quarterly,

## Chapter 6
**Fig. 6.1**: Author
**Fig. 6.2**: Chandigarh Museum Archives
**Fig. 6.3**: Author